Speak
You
Also

Speak You Also

A Survivor's Reckoning

PAUL STEINBERG

Translated by Linda Coverdale
with Bill Ford

Metropolitan Books

Henry Holt and Company   New York

Henry Holt and Company, LLC
Publishers since 1866
115 West 18th Street
New York, New York 10011

Metropolitan Books™ is an imprint of
Henry Holt and Company, LLC.

Published in Canada by Fitzhenry and Whiteside Ltd.,
195 Allstate Parkway, Markham, Ontario L3R 4T8

Originally published in France in 1996 under the title
Chronique d'ailleurs by Editions Ramsay, Paris.

Library of Congress Cataloging-in-Publication Data

Steinberg, Paul.
[Chronique d'ailleurs. English]
Speak you also : a survivor's reckoning / Paul Steinberg ;
translated by Linda Coverdale.
p.   cm.
ISBN 0-8050-6064-2 (hb.: alk. paper)
1. Steinberg, Paul.   2. Jews—France—Biography.
3. Holocaust, Jewish (1939–1945)—France—Personal narratives.
4. Auschwitz (Concentration camp)   I. Title.

DS135.F9 S7413 2000
940.53'18'092—dc21   00-028146
[B]

Henry Holt books are available for special
promotions and premiums. For details contact:
Director, Special Markets

First American Edition 2000

Designed by Paula Russell Szafranski

Printed in the United States of America

10   9   8   7   6   5   4   3   2   1

Speak, you also,
speak as the last,
have your say.

–PAUL CELAN
Translated by
Michael Hamburger

Contents

*Speak
You
Also*

Apprenticeship

I was in my junior year at the Lycée Claude-Bernard. I was almost seventeen. I'd barely made it through my first baccalaureate examination, scraping by with only one and a half points to spare.

It was September 23 and I'd just spent a few months in absolute euphoria, which might, in the year of disgrace 1943, seem hard to believe.

I'd been suffering from gambling fever for a full year, ever since one of my classmates, who was later to have a brilliant career as a racing columnist, had dragged me along with him to the Auteuil racetrack, in the Bois de Boulogne. I didn't need much persuasion. From that day on, I was hooked. I cut classes to go to the track, and during the winter, since I couldn't go all the way across Paris to the Vincennes racecourse, I counted the days until the steeplechase and flat-racing season opened again. It wasn't long before I was in hock up to my neck, to the tune of two years' spending money.

There wasn't a single school chum, friend of the family, or vague acquaintance I hadn't hit up for money, including even the

3

old Russian guy with the lending library. I'd been reduced to slinking around, and rumor had it I'd sold the family silver, which was an exaggeration: at most I'd swiped a bit of money from my father's pockets.

Things had reached this sorry pass when my day arrived. The moment of glory every player encounters once or twice in a lifetime. I was later—much later—to have two more such strokes of luck, but by then I was no longer a serious gambler, so my good fortune didn't thrill me anywhere near as much.

On the day in question, I arrived at Auteuil for the third race; I had thirty francs on me, and the infield lawn, the cheapest public enclosure, was bathed in sunshine. The race was a steeple with nine starters. I picked Kami, owned by the baron de Bourgoing, and bet ten and ten. Kami romped home at four to one.

The fourth event was the main hurdle race of the spring season. I'd made my choice long before: M. Cruz Valer's Ludovic the Moor, ridden by Bonaventure, red cap, red and yellow stripes. The horse had run three times that season without showing, and I was convinced he'd been held back for this race. He was a horse of supreme elegance. I adored the way he caressed the hedges going over them. He was a great favorite, three to one, if I recall correctly. He won by three lengths and was never even challenged. I'd bet thirty francs each way. Out of gratitude I've bet on Ludovic the Moor's offspring down to the third generation.

The fifth race was the big steeplechase for four-year-olds. I was on a roll. I chose Melik II, trained by Buquet, ridden by Dornaletche (who won once in a blue moon), ten-to-one odds. At the eighth pole water hazard, I was a little worried; Melik was in sixth place but running clear. I lost sight of the horses when they tackled the last turn by the porte de Passy and the Open Ditch, I heard shouting from the stands when someone took a spill, then the horses hurtled past me a hundred yards from the finish. Melik II, blue cap, blue and white checked silks, had a six-length lead and danced past the winning post.

I was loaded with money. I felt like I was God and that the future was up to me. In the sixth race I recognized an old acquaintance: C. V. Lombard's Kitai, eight big goose eggs his last eight times out, now at forty to one. The hour of his resurrection had come. I bet a hundred francs to place and Kitai promptly came home second, paying twice as much as the winner.

At that point I decided to call it a day. The next morning I paid my debts, cash on the barrel head. I bought all the books I wanted. I still had more than enough left for a few splurges in the near future. Except for one small hitch: the following week, I lost almost everything.

But what relief, what delight, what luck it was to live that day!

My obsession did not prevent me from keeping up with the news. The war had taken a turn for the better. Italy had switched sides, the Soviet army was running roughshod over Jerry and approaching the Polish frontier, everyone was waiting for the Allied landing, and the "collabos" were looking grim. The wind had shifted. I had long ago stopped wearing the yellow star; the turf was one reason, plus I figured it was a trap for suckers.

I wasn't a complete idiot. I'd noticed my circle gradually thinning out, I'd heard about the Vel d'hiv'* roundups, which had barely touched the posh 16th arrondissement, where I lived. I

*The Vélodrome d'hiver was an indoor bicycle arena in Paris that was used as a detention area. (All notes in this text are the translator's.)

knew that being one of the chosen people was not the fashion of the day or even of yesterday, let alone of the days to come.

My father had never bothered to talk to me about what might lie ahead. My sister was in unoccupied France with false papers, my brother had been in England since 1936. I was the youngest; my father didn't care much for me. After all, I'd killed his wife, my mother, when I was born. I loathed my stepmother.

As for my mother, I had to wait until the winter of 1992 to introduce myself to her. In East Berlin, at the old Jewish cemetery. At her tomb, clean and neat in that ravaged junkyard of families, their descendants extinguished because they burned so well. Thanks to my brother, her grave had been maintained. I brought back photos: my daughter Hélène saw her grandmother Hélène's name engraved on the plinth of gray marble.

True, a friend of the family, Mme Lurienne, had stepped in and tried to hide me with some farm people she knew in Troissereux, north of Beauvais. We'd taken the train at the Gare du Nord and then a wheezy country bus. I'd brought along my fishing pole, with which I'd been contributing to my little family's supply of protein by catching gudgeon, roach, and bleak beneath the pont Exelmans. I was sometimes joined by a classmate, Jacques Deniaud, an experienced angler who'd reel in five fish for my every one. It was my first encounter with technical skill.

Waiting for me in Troissereux was a real French family. Father, mother, their little mam'selle, and Auntie examined me suspiciously and kept me for three days, which I devoted to fishing for rainbow perch in the local pond. Then they informed Mme Lurienne that they couldn't run the risk of letting me stay, for fear of upsetting the *Kommandantur.* I packed my stuff and returned to Paris, not forgetting my fishing pole.

My best friend, Pierre Bertaux, who lived in Sèvres and in whose home I'd spent many a Sunday, could not persuade his parents to take me in, either. His father was some sort of administrative secretary in the Senate and was afraid of jeopardizing his sinecure.

And so that's how I came to set out on September 23, 1943, armed with ration coupons, to fetch our daily bread from the bakery on the boulevard Exelmans, just beyond the corner of rue Erlanger.

A few years later, in 1950, while driving north to Le Touquet, I went through Troissereux again. I allowed myself the luxury of stopping there. The farm was a bit more dilapidated. The small grocery store, which the family ran to earn a little something extra, had closed.

Mam'selle, who still was one, did not recognize me, or pretended not to. I had to explain to her that I was the boy who (and so on), that I'd been deported shortly afterward, that I'd made it back by the merest chance, and that I held her and her parents in everlasting contempt. She mumbled a few indistinct words, among which I made out the inevitable "We didn't know." I must really have spoiled her afternoon. Cold comfort.

Back at the bakery in 1943, the long arm of the law had been waiting. There were two plainclothes policemen and they were on to me. The informer's letter had been quite explicit. Times were hard: the police didn't have a car so we took the Métro. They explained to me that they were armed and would use their guns if I tried to escape. They didn't bother with handcuffs.

I suppose that in September 1943 two police officers taking a sixteen-year-old kid, probably Jewish, on the Métro in handcuffs might have aroused the ire of the working classes and that my escorts preferred to avoid embarrassment. I must have had two or three chances while our train was sitting in a station, before the doors had shut, to make a run for it. I did no such thing . . . My life would have been completely different, and I would not be writing these lines.

I think the Cité station was closed; we got out at Odéon, and there I had a strange inspiration. I asked my cops if I could duck into Librairie Maloine, a bookstore on rue de l'École-de-Médecine; I still had a tiny reserve left over from my exploits at the track, and I chose a book of analytical inorganic chemistry. I knew absolutely nothing about the subject, which was part of the first-year university curriculum for the degree in mathematics, physics, and chemistry, but I was very keen on chemistry.

M. Artigas had been my physics and chemistry teacher at Claude-Bernard for two years in a row. He was not exactly charismatic—indeed, my classmates found him frankly pathetic—but by some miracle, through some improbable channel, he'd managed to get me interested in chemistry. Only chemistry; I was a washout in physics.

Mendeleyev's table, valences, inorganic chemical reactions like $H_2SO_4 + KMnO_4$ held no secrets for me, and I haunted the science museum, the Palais de la Découverte, where I discussed rare earth metals with the head of the inorganic chemistry department. The periodic table, in color, was the sole decoration of the closet that served as my bedroom.

The book was to come with me to Drancy, the collection camp on the northeastern outskirts of Paris, and on to Auschwitz, where it was confiscated, but by then I knew it by heart, and the knowledge I'd acquired would later help save my life.

Long afterward, around 1960, a friend who was a math instructor helped me track down Artigas, who happened to be teaching in my friend's lycée. I went to see him and recounted my story. I sometimes imagine that he was deeply moved by it; I would have been, in his place. Can one conceive of a more magnificent destiny for an educator than saving someone's life through his teaching? If he was touched, he didn't show it. I did not see him again. Peace to his soul!

From Odéon we walked to police headquarters, myself in front, the cops two steps behind. We went up a few flights to a shabby office. There they went through the motions of questioning me as to the whereabouts of the rest of my tribe. I played dumb, and they didn't press me.

I was only just beginning to feel distressed. I think I had tears in my eyes at one point. I sensed, and rightly so, that I was at a turning point in my life.

They decided to take me home so I could pack a suitcase. I tried in vain to find out what was in store for me. Perhaps they hadn't a clue either! Today I tend to think they were vaguely ashamed. Ten months later, no doubt, they slipped on the armbands of the Resistance, shot off a few rounds, and continued their careers as cops. Perhaps one or the other of them even gave a thought, once or twice, to the kid they sent off to hell with his chemistry book—or maybe they forgot to bother! The virus of conscience is present in all of us, but only a few people fall ill or develop an itch from it. The rest get off scot-free.

When I got home, I was stumped: what should I take? Most of my clothes were in a second residence. In the end I packed up my pillow as well as my slippers, which were destined to play a decisive role. I've always been very attached to my pillows. The absence of the maternal breast, a psychiatrist would say. (Even today, when I enter a hotel room, the first thing I do is open the closet and feel the pillows.) I shut my suitcase. I also took along some pears that had been set to ripen on the kitchen windowsill. The policemen had stayed in the living room. That's when I had my best chance: out the kitchen door and down the service stairs. It was three flights; I could have reached the street before they'd even realized that they'd blown it. After all, I tell myself, maybe that was what they expected me to do. Who can say? I did nothing, I knew nothing—absolutely nothing. It's easy to judge in hindsight.

From the apartment they took me to the police station on boulevard Exelmans at the corner of rue Chardon-Lagache. Their day's work done, they handed me over and went home to their wives and kids. I was placed in a cell in the station basement, with the door left open. The police seemed decent enough, telling me I'd have to wait there for the prison van. I thought about the movie theater next door, L'Exelmans, which vanished ages ago and where, three years earlier, in June 1940, I'd seen a Tom Mix film that was being shown in two parts over two weeks. At the end of the first episode, Tom Mix and his horse had fallen into a trap, a pit dug by the bad guys and covered with branches. I'll never know how he got out of it because I didn't see the second half: in the meantime, the wolves had entered Paris. American movies were banned until 1944, by which time I was long gone, and in any case, they'd stopped showing Tom Mix films by then, except perhaps way out in the sticks.

At this point in my musings about the silver screen, sirens began to wail. Air-raid alert. The cops got in a tizzy over where to put me. This was the last real chance I missed. The door was open; I could have run for it, up the fifteen steps, and seen what they would do in a 400-meter dash. Perhaps, there again, they were giving me a hint, thinking, Get going, you little jerk! I considered it. I didn't do it.

Cold feet or maybe, instinctively, inexplicably, the will, the desire to go on to the bitter end, the agony I could never have suspected lay ahead.

I've often wondered if I didn't choose my fate deliberately. After all, a prisoner's vocation is to escape, even in the direst situations. I went meekly to the slaughter like a lousy sheep, and yet there were times when I could have bolted.

Of course, once I was cornered by death, I defended myself, fought back, resisted any way I could—but passively, bending before the blast. So it's hard for me to present my behavior in an honorable—let alone glorious—light.

That evening the paddy wagon came to take me to the central police station. I lined up to sign the register with a few pimps and thugs, plus the day's catch of Jews. I handed out my pears. I remember a motherly whore who told me I should keep my eats for myself.

I spent the night in cell 10, where the sons of Abraham, Moses, and Jacob passed through in procession for three years. The walls were covered with polyglot graffiti. There were five or six of us. I don't remember any of them or what was said. Maybe I was sleeping. In that department, kids have it easy.

The next morning, we were taken to Drancy.

On October 20, less than a month later, I took my first group shower at Auschwitz III–Monowitz, also known as Buna.

Naked as a jaybird, clutching some gritty soap, I was rubbing myself fore and aft under the lukewarm water when suddenly all eyes were on me, or rather, on my lower abdomen.

"What the hell are you doing here?" asked a Parisian furrier from the Poissonnière neighborhood.

I looked at him in bewilderment. He pointed at my dick, called his buddies over, and shouted, "He's not circumcised!"

I didn't know a thing about circumcision or about the Jewish religion in general. My father had neglected, through foolish prudery, no doubt, to discuss this captivating subject with me. In all likelihood I was and I remain the only uncircumcised Jew in the whole of France to be deported to Auschwitz. It had never even occurred to me to play that trump.

More and more men had gathered around me, all laughing so hard they could barely stand up. Finally, one of them informed me I was a complete and utter asshole.

Digression I

To understand, to help people understand. Everyone tries to understand, both the one who writes and the one who reads.

How to make people understand that world by reconstructing it on paper—this is the problem that faces us all, Primo Levi, Robert Frances, Jorge Semprun, and the others.

To describe the indescribable. An overweening ambition? In math class, over fifty years ago now, I tried to prove Euclid's fifth postulate. The teacher, M. Ostenc, who liked me, gently pointed out that my proof was based on a consequent of that very postulate.

And first of all, or after all, does that world even exist, even for us? Could we have lived for half a century, the rest of our lives, with that world still present in us as it was then? Surely it would have killed us.

It did kill some of us. Those who survive, like me, have found a way of dealing with it.

Preventive treatment. Mental prophylaxis.

Memory is kind to us, beneficent. It muddles certain areas, erases things here and there.

Small islands remain, specific spots, isolated, standing out starkly against murky depths our words cannot begin to fathom. The parallel universe, the one where logic, ethics, codes no longer apply and are replaced by another logic, another ethics, other codes, which we must assimilate quickly, on pain of dying even more quickly.

And that constant clash between the crushing certainty of our more or less imminent death (a certainty that was true for ninety-five percent of us) and our rage to live in spite of all obstacles, the perfectly irrational hope, the animal instinct that made us cling ferociously to life without letting go, not even for an instant, which would have proved fatal.

That we won in the end, that the death machine seized up and by some miracle allowed a few survivors to slip through the net, isn't this reason enough to believe that somehow we were different? Or rather, made different, by that very experience? We live within parentheses, a reprieve that has lasted fifty years.

Yet we are not special in any way, of course, save for the stubborn, persistent, flawless good fortune that made us the winners of this unlikely lottery. The proof is that the indestructible ones, the iron men, lasted only a few months, and among the rare survivors are a few whom none of us would have given the ghost of a chance.

My plan is to navigate among the little islands of memory that still remain. To fish for the scraps of recollection that still rise from the depths. Perhaps this risky expedition will allow me to give an account—unsettling, no doubt—of the world from which perhaps I have not escaped even after half a century.

The one thing I am sure of is that writing this will knock me off balance, deprive me of a fragile equilibrium achieved with the utmost care. This imbalance will in turn affect my writing, pushing it either toward greater bluntness or into affectation.

I might break down along the way, which is what happened the last time I tried this, in the sixties. These pages could wind up in a shoe box at the back of a cupboard.

Shoe box. Pandora's box.

I know this will be grueling, I'll have to keep an eye on myself, keep track of the catharsis. Those around me, my wife, daughters, grandson, friends, will have to live to the rhythm of my morbid moods. And yet I feel that this time I'll make it to the end. My defenses have weakened with age and so, too, my interest in ducking the issue.

I don't think I'll crack up.

The Last Fight

I met Victor Young Perez in Drancy. He was out of it, punch drunk. He'd taken a lot of blows, and even with a flyweight, the punches add up. His speech was slurred, his comprehension slow and laborious, but he was the best of fellows, kind, generous, smiling vacantly as if his eyes were still fixed on his past glory.

He hadn't fought in the ring since 1937. His last opponent, I think, must have been Valentin Angelmann, who was just beginning his career. Perez had won the World Championship back in 1934.

His winnings must have been just about gone. Boxers are more grasshoppers than ants. He'd always found it hard to hang on to money.

The police had arrested him in the working-class neighborhood of Belleville, and while they were at it, they'd rounded up his circle of admirers, who were necessarily disinterested by then. There were one or two second-string boxers, the kind who warm up the audience before the main event (I remember in particular a bantamweight, Robert Lévy, who took a liking to me), plus a manager, some sparring partners, and various young sports fans.

At the time I was a faithful reader of *L'Auto,* the *Sports Illustrated* of its day. From track and field to swimming, boxing to soccer, cycling to basketball, I followed everything devotedly. I knew Valmy's record in the 100 meters, Hansenne's in the 800. I followed the duel between Hatot and Jesum in the 100-meter freestyle: one minute, one second—a time that wouldn't even get them into the women's semifinals these days.

I thrilled to the exploits of Émile Idée and Goutorbe and was a big fan of the US Métro and Paris Université Club basketball teams, of Destremeau and Petra in tennis, of the Paris Racing Club in soccer.

So with Young Perez I was in my element.

We formed a congenial little group, wandering about in the camp, indulging in a bit of boxing horseplay now and then. Robert Lévy dealt me my first knockdown, slipping a hook beneath my straight left despite my longer reach.

We had endless discussions about the respective merits of the different types of boxers, past and present, attentive all the while to the many false rumors and optimistic fairy tales constantly circulating through Drancy. Since we were always hungry, we also talked interminably about food, and I quickly learned everything there was to know about the various couscous joints in Belleville. My new friends were all Sephardim, Perez from Tunis, the rest from Morocco.

This lasted twelve days. Twelve days of civilian and almost civil life in that place—Drancy—which, unbeknown to us, was an airlock leading from the past to what would be, for almost all of us,

18

death. Not a banal, respectable death; a different death. We probably ought to invent a different word. Decomposition? Putrescence? What term does justice to physical, psychological, and moral annihilation, experienced in wretched shame?

I can still see the Champ's mute, gentle gaze. We all called him the Champ. Hard to believe that this man had spent eight years pounding on other guys. Each punch he threw must have hurt him more than his opponent, or else he had changed completely by the time I met him.

On October 6, we learned there would be a transport the following day. That evening, we found out we'd all be going. The group of sports lovers, Philippe (who belongs to another chapter), and me.

Of course, we hadn't the foggiest idea where we were going. Theories: a ghetto, a factory, a labor camp near a mine, in Bavaria, or close to Berlin, or in Poland. We were going to be issued triple rations, we'd be given marks or zlotys.

All at once I was an essential part of the group as the only one who could speak fluent German. I was going to be the interpreter, the guide, the adviser. I was not unhappy at this increased prestige. In short, I wasn't cut out to be a follower.

They carted us off on the morning of October 7. Transport number 60. One thousand and fifty still-human beings. Fifty to a railroad car. But this journey—the shock of arrival, the fate of those who didn't go up in smoke that same day—is a story I'll tell if I feel up to it. Let's stay in this one.

When we arrived in Buna, they herded 340 of us—all males between fifteen and fifty years old, in apparent good health—into a big tent reserved for new arrivals. Registration, tattooing, basic drill in saluting, roll call, camp etiquette. Replies and responses to orders barked in German, blow-by-blow training for those slow to catch on. I did my job. I had the Champ registered as a former World Champion. I put Robert Lévy down as Champion of France; those who could do odd jobs were listed as carpenters, locksmiths, or house painters, and I put myself down as a chemist. I was one of the two or three youngest of the lot, fresh-faced and beardless, which won me some sympathy—not always of the platonic kind—among the camp dignitaries. From them, I learned virtually everything you had to know to survive as long as possible.

On the fifth day, the Champ was sent to the kitchens, the best of all possible assignments, since it guaranteed a regular supply of food. Bits of gossip I picked up here and there led me to believe that this wasn't a tribute to his athletic glory but part of a plan. I found out the very next morning what was in the works. The Champ was to get himself back into shape. Three hours of training every day. Jump rope, footwork, shadowboxing.

Digging further, I found out more. The SS were organizing a boxing competition on the *Appellplatz,* the square where roll call was held; the date scheduled was the last Sunday in October. The Champ would fight the main event, Robert Lévy the second match.

That roll-call square where, twice a day, at six in the morning and six in the evening, in ranks of five, we stood waiting—sometimes for hours, especially in the evening, after our factory work—for the SS to finish counting us, for the sum of the tallies made by each of the twenty checkers to match the exact number of detainees furnished by the records office, minus the day's dead and hospitalized inmates . . .

At my friends' request, I was designated their manager and cornerman. Since I was now an active member of the camp, I saw my trainees only in my few spare moments. We'd been assigned, according to needs and individual abilities, to different barracks and labor *Kommandos*. As for me, until the work squad of chemists was set up, I'd been detailed to a *Kommando* that unloaded wagons. We'd begun with a wagon of bricks, and my hands were already a mess.

The big Sunday arrived. A holiday. We had two Sundays off a month. A mild, gray autumn day, graced with a few fleeting rays of sunshine.

After the distribution of the morning's rations—two hundred grams of black bread, a pat of margarine, a slice of sausage—we were condemned to fast until the evening meal. The liter of hot liquid with its few lone vegetables doled out to us by the factory on working days was sorely missed.

After the morning roll call, a work detail got busy setting up the stage. A regulation ring on a dais, rows of chairs for the SS.

We'd all gotten together, the Champ, Robert Lévy, and a few others, to consider what might happen and decide what we should do. We didn't know whom we were going to find in the opposite corner: an SS man or a common criminal, well fed, a former pro or amateur boxer, one of the *Prominenz,* the internees holding the highest posts in the camp. I thought we should on no account demonstrate any clear superiority, and absolutely not make our opponents look silly. Plus manage to achieve the main thing: take as few blows as possible.

"Is it a fight or isn't it?" asked the Champ.

"It isn't a fight," I said, "it's a show we have to put on."

From the lofty height of my seventeen years (I'd had a birthday a few days earlier), I saw myself as a wise old counselor guiding a bunch of rowdy youngsters. Today I realize that if I'd told them even part of what I'd learned and figured out, they would not have believed me or trusted me anymore.

It was getting late. The show was supposed to begin at six o'clock, at nightfall. The men left to get ready. I explained to the *Blockältester*—the senior block inmate, who was in charge of the event—that I was their cornerman and interpreter, and I managed to slip to the foot of the ring.

And now, you who are reading this, shut your eyes. Try to imagine, behind your closed eyelids, the following scene. Roll-call square, as big as two football fields; in the middle, the ring, illuminated by antiaircraft searchlights. On three sides, the electrified barbed-wire fence, four meters high. Watchtowers every fifty meters, each one with a machine gun trained on the camp, on us, by the SS men on guard.

In front of the ring, two hundred SS men of all ranks, from *Standartenführer* to *Scharführer,* sitting on eight rows of precisely lined-up chairs. They've come from all the camps: Birkenau, Auschwitz I, and the fifteen or twenty more or less lethal satellite camps within a range of thirty miles.

On the opposite side of the ring, sitting on benches to point up the difference, the camp *Nomenklatura:* a hundred, maybe a hundred and fifty senior block inmates, *Kapos* (the *Kommando* bosses), all common criminals, wearing green triangles, veterans of the camp from its beginnings in 1941, murderers of every sort, out of their minds like all the other old-timers. Lording it over them, the *Lagerältester,* the senior camp inmate. A colossus over six feet tall and weighing 220 pounds, who had a habit of killing inmates as though he were swatting flies. And who was to save my skin five or six times before dying in Buchenwald, after he'd lost his prerogatives, strangled one night in his bunk by his neighbors. It took ten of them, their puny strength increased tenfold by their hatred.

A hundred yards farther back, behind a barrier guarded by *Kapos* with wooden clubs, three or four hundred deportees who preferred to see the show rather than sleep and save their strength.

If ever there was a surrealist happening beyond the wildest imagination of a Breton, a Dalí, a Magritte, it was that evening at Monowitz. When I recall what I witnessed there from my front-row seat, I despair of bringing it to life in the mind of a sane human being.

Young Perez climbed into the ring.

We'd decided to start with two rounds, leading off with warm-ups and rope skipping, an exercise at which the Champ was a virtuoso. He moved about with small steps, the rope whipping around so fast it was practically invisible; it slipped between his feet and the canvas in some miraculous fashion, now facing front, now sideways, whirling forward, then backward, a dance punctuated from time to time by a sharp clack of castanets he produced by stamping the canvas between skips. Then, after a minute's rest, a round of shadowboxing. The boxer's whole arsenal: straight lefts, uppercuts, hooks, jabs, bobbing and weaving, advancing on the imaginary opponent, drawing back, sidestepping.

Instead of the success we'd counted on, the performance received barely a smattering of polite applause. Clearly, our monstrous audience had come not to see our choreographic display but to claim its ration of blood and violence, which was exactly what we were trying to avoid.

Perez came over and sat down on his stool. I was beside him with only a sponge, a bucket, a glass, and a towel. The Champ had been a natural flyweight. I don't remember the weight limits very well anymore, but when he was in fighting trim, he must have weighed in at around 105, 110 pounds. Although he'd developed a bit of belly since then, the Occupation, Drancy, the journey, and two weeks in a concentration camp had taken care of that. He was in good shape.

There was a stir in the opposite corner and our opponent stepped over the ropes. My jaw dropped. A beefy middleweight, around 165 pounds, just under six feet tall. I later found out he was a soldier from the Wehrmacht who'd had a few fights as an amateur.

He was white, a clotted-cream white that set off the dark blue of his trunks. Strangely, his forearms were hairy while his chest was smooth; I figured he must have shaved himself.

He had no bulging muscles and even appeared slightly flabby. I hoped he'd prove short-winded. He seemed worried.

I'd seen a number of American films about boxing and they supplied my advice to the Champ, who probably knew much better than I what he should do.

"Make him run," I said. "At least for the first two minutes of the round, dodge him, keep to the best side depending on whether he's right-handed or a lefty. Take a few punches on the gloves—the crowd will really go for the sound it makes. At the last minute, sneak under his guard and pop him one or two in the breadbasket." (I liked that expression a lot; I'd lifted it from an Errol Flynn movie.)

The Champ nodded. The referee, a big blond SS man, called the fighters to the middle of the ring. Then the bell rang.

Snow White planted himself in the center of the ring and let loose a left as long as a cavalry lance. The Champ began his scalp dance, two steps forward to draw a hook that would have felled an ox, a step to the side soliciting a straight right, then a pivot. We were lucky, the guy wasn't a southpaw, a type the Champ didn't much care for. This one was slow, you could see his moves coming a long way off.

Catching him off balance, the Champ even tried a cross to the chin, a brave but hopeless attempt—he would have needed a stepladder.

Toward the end of the round Perez snuck under the guy's guard to land a light hook to the liver, probably just to please me, which he certainly did. I found myself shouting, "Back off, back off!" If that big lug had wrapped his arms around the Champ, he could easily have strangled him. The bell rang for the one-minute break. The Champ sat down, not even breathing hard. I offered him a glass of water, which he refused, and I fanned him with my towel, the way I'd seen corners do in those boxing films.

During the second round, which went the same way, the Champ was given a warning for ducking low. Since he was five feet tall facing a middleweight, any ducking would obviously have to be low. On the other hand, his opponent found himself on the canvas after failing to connect on a bolo punch that threw him off balance. In passing the Champ handed him a series of hooks to the ribs. At the bell, the Champ told me, "Don't worry, kid, he's not so tough."

The third round began. The poor soldier was puffing like a grampus and sweating in spite of the cool evening air. My heart stopped for a moment when Perez let himself be trapped on the ropes and his opponent got those long arms around him. The strange couple waltzed a few steps like that, then Perez wriggled from his grasp like an eel and ducked behind him. He told me later he'd done it on purpose to see the guy's face up close. The bell rang one last time and the referee delivered his verdict: a tie. I decided not to play the role of a manager who's been robbed blind. Nobody hissed. The Champ slipped on his robe, I unlaced his gloves, and he stepped from the ring to make way for his buddy and the next match.

The second bout pitted my pal Robert Lévy, a natural bantamweight at 117 pounds, against a real heavyweight. An SS *Unterscharführer,* or corporal. This one looked mean, and I had to beg Robert to be careful. He'd watched the Champ's fake fight with me and, his competitive spirit roused, he wanted to go the retired boxer one better, as he himself had still been in action not six months before under the professional name of Kid Bob.

I remember that he breathed through his nose as he boxed, producing a constant, strange background noise like the chuffing of a small locomotive. He didn't have the Champ's class but he was a good worker in the ring, with a quick eye. He did his best through the first two rounds, avoiding most of the blows raining down on him, taking the others on the gloves or the arms. Punches on the arms can be painful; they tend to make you drop your guard.

In the third round Robert grew bolder and tried to land his hook, the one I'd felt in Drancy. The German had chosen to fight from a crouch, which meant that he was almost at the right height. The hook hit home, but Robert was too close and he took a head butt that was more or less deliberate; blood started pouring from his nose. The bell rang soon afterward. I tried to stop the bleeding with my towel while the referee gave the victory to the SS on points. It was Robert who consoled me, seeing me upset by all that blood.

"Nothing's broken," he said. "I've got a glass nose—you breathe on it and it gushes like a fountain!"

The show was over as far as we were concerned. I don't know what happened after that. The three of us left, my pals to go shower and put on their striped pajamas, me to return to my block, number 3.

It was time for the evening soup. The senior block inmate, Willi, had a soft spot for me and fairly often gave me an extra ladleful. I knew the cardinal rule of survival: sleep, sleep. The constant priority was to conserve your energy; looking for extra food came second. Exhaustion kills before starvation.

Ten days later, the Champ was kicked out of the kitchens: he didn't understand the orders they gave him. No one was there to translate. He wound up in a block far from mine and in a really hard *Kommando* assigned to digging ditches and laying pipe. I must have seen him again no more than twice. He was melting away. Only his smile was left; his gentle gaze, more and more absent, was already elsewhere. I think he died in January, quickly, like a snuffed-out candle.

The main sports stadium in Tunis is named after Young Perez. The small shopkeepers of the medina of Hammamet, with whom I chatted every day one August forty years later, knew that he was a famous boxer, a national hero. About his life, his death—they didn't know a thing. I wasn't tempted to fill them in.

Robert Lévy lasted a bit longer; I must have run into him by chance here and there. He, too, was in a deadly *Kommando*. He isn't listed among our thirty-five survivors in 1945. Where did he die, when and how? I can't say.

We'd left feelings and friendships by the wayside. Withdrawn inside himself, each man was fighting for his own survival. The dehumanizing machine had worked like a charm. Our existence had been reduced to vileness and humiliation.

The Life and Death of Philippe

I met Philippe Hagenauer the day after my arrival in Drancy. He was six months older than I was, born into an old Jewish family from Alsace. His father was a reporter on the daily newspaper *L'Aurore*. We were both of us bewildered, entirely on our own for the first time and anxious to escape from our loneliness.

We became fast friends in no time, as only the very young can do. We were so inseparable that people soon took us for brothers.

All this was of course the result of chance. We had found ourselves assigned to the same floor of the same raw concrete building.* We had both needed something to cling to. Fate brought us together; different surroundings might very well have created different ties.

*Drancy was a huge public-housing complex still under construction. The authorities surrounded it with chicken wire and lodged the detainees in the unfinished apartments.

We quickly acquired an entourage. I brought him into Young Perez's orbit, which offered a welcome change from the acute depression and despair that tormented our elders in Drancy. We formed a joyous group, boisterous and carefree. The unhappy detainees felt a certain fondness for us: we took their minds off their misfortune. It didn't seem possible to them that the future could be so dark when we were treating everything so lightly.

For his part, Philippe dragged me along to visit acquaintances of his family, intellectuals who beamed benevolently at us from the heights of their wisdom. And so I witnessed several debates on the comparative merits of some contemporary philosophers and heard for the first time about Jean-Paul Sartre.

Others discussed music, art, history.

The main topics of conversation were obviously the progress of the war, the imminence of the Allied landing, our chances of being liberated before the "transport." Added to all that were the rumors popping up everywhere in camp like mushrooms. First you'd hear the Resistance was going to prevent the trains from leaving, then you'd be told about a bombing raid planned for a specific time to encourage a mass escape.

Those who were more practical organized classes in German and even Polish.

Drancy seemed to me like a huge beehive in which the insects went around in circles, baffled, from one paroxysm to another. There weren't enough hours in the day to deal with all the meaningless obligations we created for ourselves.

Evenings were spent trying to pick up London on a few smuggled-in radios: the Free French were addressing the French people, and we hadn't yet realized we no longer belonged among them.

This dizzying existence went on for two weeks. I remember it almost with affection, like those old soldiers who ramble on endlessly about the joys of army life.

Then the departure of the transport was announced, and we were on it. I have no memory of that last night in Drancy. We probably slept, Philippe and I, in our innocence, as did the boxers, heedless of the future. What indelibly marked the end of my stay, however, was a nail. A nail in my shoe that finally caused an infected wound, an abscess that made me so mad I threw away the offending shoe and had to leave, travel, and arrive in slippers, limping all the way.

In the early morning, we assembled, each of us carrying a single piece of luggage, here a leather suitcase plastered with stickers from palatial international hotels, there a cardboard box tied any old which way with string. We were 1,050 men and women over fifteen years of age, including some invalids, a few pregnant women, and a good number of elderly people whose long lives would be cut short.

The Paris transport authority had supplied a caravan of 1930 Renault buses with open platforms at the rear. Each bus was loaded to capacity, the platform reserved for an armed SS guard. I seem to remember that they didn't make us pay a fare. As I write these lines I realize that for fifty years now, though I've taken the Métro thousands of times, I have never taken another Paris bus. One passes beneath my windows every ten minutes. Strange what you find, peeling away layers of behavior . . .

The drivers were surely fine people, family men doing their jobs. That day they'd been assigned a run outside their usual routes. I wonder how they felt about that day, and the ones after it, and the ones after the war, when they learned that they had provided the first lap of our journey and that four days later two out of three of their passengers went up in smoke.

Philippe and I had stayed together; we had each written, with a borrowed pencil, a short letter to a close relative to say that we were going and did not know where. I tossed the two letters through the half-open window of the bus as it headed to the suburban railroad station at Bobigny. Some kind soul picked mine up, stuck on a stamp, and mailed it: my letter reached its destination. I don't know what happened to Philippe's. Perhaps it's in the family archives somewhere and, like a new kind of message in a bottle, has touched the heart of some grand-nephew. Maybe a kid made it into a paper boat and sent it sailing off down a gutter.

The buses lined up one behind the other inside the Gare de Bobigny. We were hustled out, rather roughly.

In front of us, a classic freight train, capacity forty men per car or eight horses side by side. They packed us in, fifty to a boxcar, watched over by the SS, the French security police, and the railway employees.

The first ones inside stood against the walls of the car, luggage jealously kept within arm's reach. The last ones in, Philippe and I among them, found places in the middle. There was enough room to breathe and even to take a few steps, without treading on people, to reach the two barred ventilation ports at eye level, through which we could glimpse the world we'd left behind.

In one corner of the car was a tub hidden behind a blanket, where we were to relieve ourselves. Modesty was still part of our social conventions.

The train sat motionless for hours. I remember a distinguished-looking elderly couple. The man was a diamond merchant, I believe. They'd been rounded up in Nice. Before the war the husband had traveled on the luxurious Train Bleu, in the sleeping cars. He had never, it seemed, ridden in second class, and he said that in life one should always stick to extremes. I really liked that dictum, which I have adopted as my own.

Our traveling companions weren't exactly in a laughing mood. A few women were crying, in little stifled sobs. When the door to the freight car was closed, with an iron bar laid across it, we felt we'd been cut off from the world. The train began moving, and as night fell, the last images of the outskirts of Paris gradually disappeared.

I fell asleep. From time to time, Philippe would place a hand on my shoulder and tell me the names of the stations: Compiègne, Saint-Quentin, Valenciennes. My childhood had been oriented toward the Midi, in the south of France; my family had a home in Juan-les-Pins. This was the first time I'd ever been north of Paris.

The train halted three or four times. Once, there was a disturbance and shots were fired. It seems that some bold fellows had managed to saw through the floorboards of their car and a few men had escaped. We were assured they had been killed. Our traveling companions appeared convinced that perfect discipline and absolute docility were certain to satisfy our escorts and might even win us more favorable treatment. There were no freedom fighters in our group.

As time went by, in this sealed boxcar transferring us from one universe to another, Philippe and I spun our own little cocoon. We told each other our stories, whispering so as not to disturb our sleeping neighbors.

Philippe had enjoyed a happy childhood in the bosom of a family that had been assimilated for generations. An only son, protected and beloved; a country house on the Norman coast; an apartment in the chic section of the 17th arrondissement, over by the parc Monceau. He'd been about to begin university studies in the humanities. He saw his past as placidly uneventful and was quite curious about mine.

I no longer recall what things I confided to him or in what order I disclosed them. I don't know anymore; I can't recover the way I looked at myself at the time, a view without detachment, perspective. I considered my personal history with some confusion, and doubtless felt the need to improve my image, even if I had to distort it outrageously.

If H. G. Wells and his time machine were to send me back to Philippe's side, in that doomed car carrying future phantoms condemned to wander without sepulcher, that freight car where I no longer have my place, I who am still made of flesh and blood (however spent), here is what I would tell him, though my words would probably be quite different from those I spoke so many years ago.

If my sister and the few rare witnesses to my childhood are to be believed, I must have been a somewhat difficult little boy. I was shy, proud (according to those who loved me—vain, according to those who did not), and untruthful, more from flights of imagination than from vice. In short, a pathological liar.

Remember, I'd been bundled around from country to country: Germany, Italy, France, Spain, France again—that is to say, Berlin, San Remo, Juan-les-Pins, Paris, Barcelona, and back to Paris. Four countries, four languages, ten different homes, five schools, ten years' worth of disruptions, aborted friendships, hostile environments.

My scholastic debut took place in Juan-les-Pins, in the primary school that today still overlooks the pine forest between the Hôtel Alba, since vanished, where we'd set up house, and an orchard invaded during recess and ruthlessly plundered of figs, whose sweetish smell comes back to me even now.

I did not speak a word of French. The kids walloped me black and blue, calling me a "dirty Boche." Thus encouraged, I must have made dazzling progress, for three months later, at the arrival of a new refugee, I was able to join in and thrash him joyously with the rest.

I remember my first teacher, who put me in the corner the day I arrived for not having placed the acute accent on the line of *es* copied out in my notebook. I'd taken the accent of the example on the blackboard for a stray chalk mark, as there are no accents on German *es*.

After Juan-les-Pins, there was Paris (three homes, two schools), then Barcelona, where my father hoped to find the right climate in which to regain his lost fortune.

The outbreak of civil war inconveniently put an end to this valiant effort and we returned to France, our tails drooping, leaving our worldly possessions behind in a furniture warehouse, where they remained in storage until 1945. I'd barely begun to adjust and to hold my own in scuffles with the neighborhood kids. I belonged to an anarchist gang and would shout lustily, *"Eviva Durrutti!"*

Back in Paris, we played musical apartments again; I waltzed from Lycée Michelet to École Saint-Joseph to Jeanson-de-Sailly, where I repeated sixth grade after unwisely skipping fifth.

It was at Jeanson that I experienced my first racist attack, from an instructor—I remember as though it were yesterday. His name was Ramon. The bastard must have been a Fascist and he really had it in for me. Right in the middle of study hall, he called me *Heimatlos:* homeless, stateless, in other words, human rubbish. I was absolutely furious, and helpless. What can you do when you're eleven years old? You can remember.

Our perpetual migrations finally ended when we settled on rue Michel-Ange. I started seventh grade at the Lycée Claude-Bernard when it opened in 1938.

I lived through those years taking refuge in books. My father's collection of German works and the Parisian municipal library were at my disposal, and I indiscriminately gobbled up Shakespeare, Victor Hugo, Tolstoy, Oscar Wilde, all of Dumas, including even *Ange Pitou; or, Taking the Bastille.*

I had two bedside books I was always rereading, *The Life of Disraeli,* by André Maurois, and Dmitry Merezhkovsky's *The Romance of Leonardo da Vinci,* bound in soft black leather—I can still feel its grain in the palm of my hand. These books were to disappear during the war. After the liberation nothing remained in the apartment, stripped bare and under seal, except an Old Testament left lying in the middle of the living room floor. Isn't it funny where humor crops up?

I had to wait until I was fifteen to hear from my sister's lips, as we strolled together along the arcades of boulevard Exelmans, that my mother, whom I detested, was in reality only my stepmother. She had made this unearned promotion a condition of her marriage to my father, who'd given in without thinking twice.

My real mother, carried off by an attack of eclampsia a few days after my birth, was awaiting my visit to the Jewish cemetery in

Berlin to become better acquainted with me. The revelation was a huge relief: no longer a monster worthy of the House of Atreus, I fell into the more common and less glorious category of a Poil de Carotte.*

I was the youngest child. My brother, eight years my senior, had fled the family trap at eighteen and gone to Great Britain, where he did very well for himself.

My sister, who alone enjoyed my father's love, had celebrated her first quarter century by negotiating her independence. Between her and our stepmother reigned a sort of permanent status quo based on an established balance of power.

In 1941, my sister was arrested and spent almost a year in the Cherche-Midi prison in Paris. My father eventually pried her free by bribing a German officer with dollars. She finally found refuge in the Unoccupied Zone with false papers.

The last one left in Paris was the youngest, incapable of taking his own destiny in hand in the absence of responsible adults.

Caught between two worlds, I'd had a rough childhood and adolescence. My family lived in the closed universe of Russian refugees. I don't think I ever saw a French visitor in our home on rue Michel-Ange, except for my friends from school.

We ate lots of borscht, croquettes Pozharsky, kasha, cucumbers Malassol, and herring blinis, with caviar on special occasions. Russian grocery stores, Russian restaurants flourished on every street corner. The neighborhood of Auteuil was a little Saint-Petersburg-on-the-Seine.

*"Carrottop" is the hero of Jules Renard's tale of a sweet boy who is cruelly mistreated by his stepmother.

Our life was like something out of Nabokov. The ladies formed passionate and eternal friendships that exploded into violent scenes and ended with the women falling out forever, only to be reconciled amid laughter, hugs, tears, and lavish amounts of vodka.

The gentlemen gravely discussed politics among themselves or ritually aired their memories and homesickness while playing chess on the board, even now before my eyes, that my father and Trotsky played on in Munich in 1904 and that constitutes the bulk of my inheritance.

All this was washed down with oceans of *thé citron,* glasses of tea—*tchachkou tchai*—accompanied by the indispensable slice of lemon. The morning glass of tea that opened your eyes after a night's slumber, the glass on a winter's afternoon that warmed the marrow of your bones, the one in summer, iced, an oasis of coolness. The one on Sunday afternoon, convivial companion to the Jewish poppy-seed cake or the *vatrouchka,* the cheese-filled open tartlet.

The *tchachka tchai* was the one constant that bound together my childhood wanderings.

My parents embarrassed me: they spoke with an impossible accent. Going to the market with them was an ordeal; as for administrative formalities at police headquarters to renew identity cards and residence permits, when all we had was a passport for stateless persons, that was hell. The clerks at the windows treated us with obvious contempt: we were foreign trash of the worst variety.

Leaving the house, I changed worlds: school buddies, their parents, sports, studies. In the lycée, I was a natural goof-off. Since no one bothered to supervise my schooling, I worked when I wanted to, when I'd decided to challenge myself or if I liked the teacher.

Some faculty members couldn't stand me, others gave me the benefit of the doubt, a few considered me a prize pupil.

At the age of fourteen, in 1941, on an evening when life seemed blacker than usual to me, I decided to end it all. An authentic and straightforward suicide. From the family medicine chest I selected a small bottle labeled "Sugar of lead—Poison—For external use only." I poured what was left of the contents into some lemonade sweetened with two sugar cubes filched from the monthly ration. I swallowed it down and wrote a letter intended to pursue my father and the woman I still believed to be my mother to the grave, like the staring eye that follows Cain in Victor Hugo's poem. Then I went to bed and to what I believed would be my eternal rest.

The next morning, I awoke without even a stomachache. I had just enough time to tear up the letter, drink my tea, and dash off to school.

This belated examination of my childhood makes me realize something that escaped me all those years and that now seems blindingly obvious.

It had all been anticipated, methodically put into place: I had the advantage of an intensive and extensive preparation for life in a concentration camp. A kind of immersion course. It's all there: the continual displacements and readjustments, the absence of ties and enduring friendships, a hostile environment. Unable to rely on any outside support, I was trained for solitary combat.

I would "attend" Auschwitz with invisible resources that vastly increased my chances of survival, resources that included even my linguistic abilities, since German was my mother tongue, so to speak, and French my vernacular, while English was the language

I had spoken with my brother and studied successfully in school. Finally, Russian was the rule with my father, sister, and the usurpress, and I was literally at home in it.

It seems certain that a happy, stable childhood, protected and full of affection, would have been the worst thing I could have had.

But I wouldn't claim that this is true for everyone.

The next day, it was Belgium, then Cologne; in the evening, the station at Bielefeld, where Hitler Youth pelted us with stones.

The day after that, the crossing of Germany: Hanover, then the outskirts of Berlin. There were air-raid sirens and searchlights. We saw flames, ruins. Struck by pikes and banderillas, the beast was staggering but not yet down, and it was too early for the muleta and the sword. At Hanover, we'd been given some water. We were supposed to have provisions enough for three days. Some people had rationed themselves carefully and ate at fixed times, while others had devoured everything in a day and a half and were reduced to scrounging.

We waited for several hours in Breslau; a track had been cut, and the train was put into reverse. Then we headed again toward the east; those who knew their geography announced our entrance into Silesia. Two or three people were back in their native land, from which they had extricated themselves with some difficulty more than twenty years before and to which they were now returning free of charge.

Philippe lived each day as it came, without worrying about the next one, or at least he pretended as much. He cheered me up when I needed it. My imagination was boiling over. I must have concocted a hundred prophetic scenarios, none of which came even remotely close to what we were going to live through and die of.

On the morning of the third day, the tenth of October, the train stopped. We were in what looked like a station, in open country. We could hear a great commotion outside, brief orders shouted in German. Standing at the tiny ventilation opening, I saw men in blue and white zebra stripes running everywhere and German soldiers, probably SS men, some of them with fearsome guard dogs on leashes.

We heard the unbolting of the freight car door; daylight streamed into the shadows where we'd just spent three days. *"Raus, raus,"* we heard. "Leave your luggage!" Philippe and I jumped down first, with me hopping on one foot: my abscess was coming to a head and I couldn't walk very well. We tried to help the elderly but an SS guard hustled us along: *"Schnell, in die Reihe."* Hurry up, get in line.

Our car was the third or fourth on the train; they were already opening the doors of the last ones. Before us stretched a line of two or three rows about fifty yards long. Family members held one another's hands, arthritic oldsters clinging for better or worse to their offspring. A few kids who were on their own had latched onto makeshift parents. A society had formed itself in continuity with the past. This society had ten minutes, five minutes, one minute left before absolute collapse and the ultimate voyage. Soon there must have been six or seven hundred people behind us. I told Philippe that we'd be better off up front, that those at the end ran the risk of waiting in line for nothing.

I had my arm wrapped around his neck and leaned on him to ease the pain in my foot. We arrived in front of three SS officers.

Philippe was sent to the line on the left. The oldest officer, the one in the middle—I later found out he was Mengele—asked me, *"Was ist mit dem Fuss, gebrochen?"* What's wrong with your foot? Is it broken?

"Nein, Herr Offizier, ein Abszess an der Fusssohle." No, sir, an abscess on the sole.

He looked at me, surprised by my accent, consulted one of his henchmen with a glance, and sent me off to rejoin Philippe in the line of the living. The line on the right, with the exception of a few young women, never saw another sunrise.

They packed us into trucks. I saw the striped pajamas piling up the suitcases. I'd abandoned mine like everyone else. Good-bye, pillow! The only thing I'd saved, stashed under my jacket, was the chemistry book, which I'd learned practically by heart at Drancy. Philippe had saved a toothbrush and the short stories of Voltaire. A few words exchanged with the blue-and-whites had led me to suspect that we stood a good chance of winding up in the same clothes the next day. The pajamas reminded me of the Paris Racing Club colors, but the thought wasn't much comfort.

The trucks had begun to move. We went through villages, past bare fields and factories; it was a short trip. We arrived at a big gate guarded by SS men. Dogs barked briefly. The gate opened: we saw barbed-wire fences, watchtowers, a large, empty square, a series of low wooden buildings, and men in blue and white just about everywhere. The trucks slammed on their brakes. We piled out and were made to run down a hallway. Some detainees told us in German, a few others in French, "Hand over all your belongings, you can't keep them, you'll come get them later." And that's how it was. I left my book with a doctor, a camp inmate, who was to remember this later on. At the end of the hallway there was a large room. The order came: *"Alles ausziehen."* Take everything off. Three hundred and forty guys stark naked—I'd never seen anything like that, it was a little silly. Some positioned their hands as fig leaves, others hunched themselves over. No one was laughing. The next stage was the shower, hot, with a poor excuse for soap. If we'd known what taking a shower meant for those sent to the right back at the station, we'd have had a miserable time of it.

After the shower, we went in single file past men in the clothing storerooms who picked out and handed to each of us a pair of long johns and a shirt, then a jacket, a pair of pants, and a cap—all three with blue and white stripes—plus a pair of big, clumsy shoes with heavy wooden soles.

The men sized us up like tailors, which most of them had been on the outside. We wound up with clothes that more or less fitted us. Some were lucky enough to get relatively clean garments made in the camp workshops; others inherited patchworks of rags. There were no belts, so holding up our pants, driven forward by the yells of men we would later find in charge of our fate (*Kapos,* senior block inmates, and their assistants, the *Stubendienst*—all SS lackeys), we trotted into the *salon de coiffure.*

Standing behind a row of stools, the local barbers waited, clippers in hand. It took about two minutes to turn our heads into cue balls. When I got out of there I looked around and saw Philippe; I had to look twice. Before me stood not Philippe but a gallows bird no respectable citizen would want to meet up with on a lonely road. I must have given him the same impression. We tried to smile at each other. Our hearts weren't in it.

At the end of our tour, we each received a chipped red mess tin and the warning, *"Ohne Schüssel, keine Suppe."* No bowl, no soup. With the tin came a spoon we would learn to sharpen on one edge of the handle, making a knife to cut our morning bread.

Turned out by the assembly line, the spitting image of the standard prisoner, the *Häftling,* we were herded along to our home, the large tent where we would spend the next week in training for camp life.

The tent was a vast temporary shelter housing rows of three-tiered wooden bunks. In the front was a protected and thus off-limits area reserved for the senior block inmate and his assistants. It was before this sacred enclosure that our food would be doled out. We formed our own groups: in my bunk bay were the boxers, Philippe, an older boy named Hirsch, who had tagged along with the group since Drancy, plus two or three others whose names and faces I can't recall anymore.

The bunks had sailcloth mattresses, which had been stuffed with straw through a side opening, lying on loosely joined planks, which meant those in the lower bunks frequently received wisps of straw and other debris right in the face. There were also a pillow made like the mattress and two blankets, one of which served as the sheet.

The first object lesson given us was in *Bettenbauen,* the "construction" of the bed. We had to learn how to produce in five minutes—timed with a watch—a bed that was neatly squared away: mattress smoothed out evenly, blanket folded like a step at a crisp right angle over a pillow plumped into a perfect cube. With a single gesture, the *Stubendienst* behind us would tear apart every unsatisfactory job. This went on for two hours. It became clear that some of us were allergic to architecture and would never succeed in building a proper bed. Others, however, were particularly gifted and became specialists, making beds for the less gifted in return for a modest payment in kind. We were all busily practicing when an order rang out: *"Aufhören!"* Stop! Then, *"Anstehen!"* Line up! A big shot surrounded by his retinue had entered the tent, a giant with the shoulders of a furniture mover. He was elegantly dressed in a black jacket with his badge of office (a green triangle), gleaming black boots, and a visored cap of the sort motorists wore in 1920.

He slowly reviewed our ranks, studying us attentively. He stopped in front of me and looked at my feet, for I'd managed to get my slippers back: *"Was ist mit dir los, woher hast du Pantoffeln?"* What's the matter with you? Where'd you get those slippers?

I replied in my best Berliner accent. Unaware of whom I was addressing, I spoke without any marked signs of respect. He'd gotten out of bed on the right side: he chuckled. Others, in different circumstances, were beaten and kicked to death on the spot.

"Woher sprichst du Deutsch, Junge?" How come you speak German, kid?

"Ich bin ein geborener Berliner." I was born in Berlin.

Then he told me to go to the *Krankenbau,* the camp infirmary, to have my wound dressed, and said we'd meet again. This was my first stroke of luck. I'd sweet-talked the *Lagerältester.* The formidably dangerous senior camp inmate.

The next day was devoted to learning various rituals and, above all, the salutes. We were taught the *Mützen auf, Mützen ab,* the basic exercise that served as a common denominator in all the camps.

In the presence of an SS soldier you had to stand at attention and doff your cap, *Mützen ab,* slapping it against your thigh; it was the same for roll call. The command equivalent of "At ease!" was

Mützen auf, "Caps on." If an SS man spoke to you, or even looked at you, you had to salute and recite your identification, that is, the number that would be assigned to you and tattooed on your left arm, the number that from then on would be your official identity.

The tattooing took place the following day, in fact, at the hands of the approved expert. We lined up for the last time in alphabetical order. Our series began with 156,900 and something. Philippe was baptized 157,090 and I became 157,239. It was all done with the same needle, a succession of rather deep shots, painful but bearable. (I've never experienced unbearable pain. Unless it was last year—and morphine managed to take care of it.) Just my bad luck, my family name started with *S,* which came right after the *R*s. And someone who had a last name beginning with that letter had a hepatitis virus. I was infected along with thirty or forty others who had no antibodies. The epidemic broke out after a few weeks' incubation, and I'm probably the only one who survived it.

Meanwhile, the senior block boss and the *Stubendienst* had harangued us several times, telling us everything we urgently needed to know. The speeches were in German, sprinkled with terms specific to the language of the concentration camps. This information was lost on most of the listeners, and I was in charge of translating and interpreting it for my friends and acquaintances. I'd managed to get on the good side of a dwarf *Stubendienst,* a former circus acrobat and juggler, strong as a tiny Turk, and his benevolence had earned me, on the eighteenth of October, my seventeenth birthday, a second liter of soup, dredged from the bottom of the pot, where it was thickest. He taught me the ropes; I picked up almost everything it was vital to know. It was this same dwarf who, in a fit of anger months later, more than half strangled Primo Levi, newly arrived and attending camp school in the tent, as we had done.

Speaking with the hindsight of this past half century, I think that I had an intuitive and acute understanding of that parallel universe in which we had been stranded. I figured out its antilogic, its laws.

These rules became clear only much later, as the decantation of the group removed its most vulnerable members in a strict order. The original 340 of us were reduced by forty percent in three months; by sixty percent in eight months, since the summer is less lethal than the winter; by eighty-five percent after a year. The last fifteen percent formed an irreducible remainder because they were adapted to life in the camp and benefited from various advantages. Only the unusual events linked with the evacuation of Auschwitz reduced their number to a handful of survivors.

It seemed immediately obvious to me that we were a herd, no longer individuals, that we were despised as a group for being new, doomed, the lowest of the low, and that those who would break free would be exceptional cases—doctors, boxers, and perhaps a few subjects selected at the whim of the lords of power.

Because in any flock of sheep or goats, the herdsman always has his favorite.

To survive you had to try to adapt yourself—and be able to make the adjustment. Which right from the outset was impossible for highly structured personalities, men in their forties with social standing, a sense of dignity, men who couldn't accept that communication from on high to us, the bottom, came only through blows and insults.

Those who rebelled were crushed on the spot. This was the category of immediate victims, the first layer, which also furnished the rare cases of suicide.

Next to go were the sentimental ones, those who worried day and night about their wives, their elderly parents, their children, whose fate they did not yet know. These people were eaten up by anguish, which sapped their resistance.

In a subcategory were those who despaired, the pessimists, those who saw no way out, because they had no will to live. These men let themselves die, passively, through gradual degradation, until the final selection.

Material factors obviously played a role. Work conditions, first and foremost.

Given the above, it should have been possible to sketch a profile of the deportee most likely to survive. All you had to do was list the advantages he needed and the crippling flaws that would disqualify him. *Modus vivendi* . . . of a hitherto unknown type.

The results of this quantitative analysis are ambiguous. The sole common denominator of the survivors seems to me to be an inordinate appetite for life—and the flexibility of a contortionist. I don't believe in the steadfast hero who endures every trial with his head held high, the tough guy who never gives in. Not in Auschwitz. If such a man exists, I never met him, and it must be hard for him to sleep with that halo.

It was much too soon, in that dawning realization, to assess my own chances of survival, to take stock of any assets I had that would help me bear up. Too soon as well to anticipate the fate of Philippe and my other friends.

I was fully aware that I was alone, that I would have to fight for life on my own. That the struggle would leave me no resources to help my friends was something I would not learn until later, when I'd hit rock bottom.

In the tent, at the beginning of that ordeal, I was still carrying the ballast of a full range of human feelings: friendship, compassion, solidarity. After they'd gone by the board, it would be a long while before I retrieved them again, too late for the friends of my first days, but in time for a few others I'd made along the way.

I did not translate for my companions the fateful sentences that ended most official pronouncements: *"In sechs Wochen seit ihr alle Muselmänner. Von hier geht es nur durch den Schornstein raus."* In six weeks you'll all be "Muslims." The only way out of here is up the chimney.

Through I don't know what linguistic aberration, *Muselmänner* in camp slang meant inmates you knew were not long for this world.

My friends did learn that we were in Auschwitz III–Monowitz, or Buna, a camp of about ten thousand men young enough and fit enough to work; that we were meant to provide cheap labor, for any and all jobs, for I. G. Farben, the giant chemical concern of the Third Reich; that the factory was designed to make the synthetic rubber the Wehrmacht desperately needed; that we would be assigned to *Kommandos* according to our abilities and professions, either as specialists or as common workers, which last would be used for the heavy labor. That sounded the death knell for lawyers, merchants, teachers, civil servants—an early rehabilitation of the manual trades. An exception was made for doctors, with which our convoy was abundantly provided. I heartily recommend to future candidates for deportation that they enter the medical and paramedical professions, which lead to cushy camp jobs and various perks.

And so Drs. Waitz, Ohrenstein, Feldbaum, and a few others were the first to find niches. Waitz survived . . .

I found out that we were the first French convoy sent to Monowitz; the others had wound up at Auschwitz II–Birkenau or Auschwitz I, where the outlook was even grimmer.

We had been preceded by the Jews of Salonika (whose agony had been appalling, and only a handful of whom survived the trip), two Dutch convoys, a few hundred Danish, the Polish overflow from overcrowded Treblinka and Majdanek, some German Jews, Austrians who had survived the terrible years of 1941–43 (some of whom held enviable jobs), a few Russian survivors of prisoner-of-war camps who had already lived through hell, some Gypsies, Jehovah's Witnesses, and homosexuals. All of them wore square or triangular badges in distinctive colors.

A small minority of political prisoners was concentrated around several havens of power: the *Schreibstube,* or camp secretariat, and the kitchen. These prisoners did not run the camp, as in Dachau and Buchenwald; in Auschwitz, the SS saw to it that power was in the hands of common criminals. Still, the "politicals" had some hidden influence, which they occasionally used on behalf of their Party comrades.

After the tattooing, we were registered. Number, nationality, profession. From among those who had been graduated from lycées, I gathered a clan of fake chemists and, just in case, for several evenings in a row I gave lessons in inorganic chemistry, which I had studied, whereas I knew nothing about organic chemistry, not even the formula for benzene. Since our training was over, we were about to be put on the market.

Meanwhile, we had tasted the joys of morning and evening roll call, standing in front of the tent in ranks of five. The weather was still mild, not even rainy. We'd stand for an hour, or two, or three. The veterans had told us of roll calls lasting up to twelve hours after an escape attempt or when there was a public hanging.

It was in the tent, during those days of idleness interrupted by bullying and hazing, that I committed the only real theft of my life. The dwarf *Stubendienst* who had taken a shine to me would summon me from time to time to keep him company in the room reserved for the "staff." One day when I was alone with him he was called away for some reason and I found myself gazing at a dozen fresh whole loaves of black bread, smelling sweetly of baking, ready for distribution the following day.

Hunger, true hunger, is an indescribable feeling that erupts all the more violently when the mind is at liberty and the body at rest. Then it becomes an obsession. During those initial days in the camp, before we had grown used to permanent undernourishment, when we could still remember our previous existence, I saw men in their prime weep from hunger.

Tantalized, I gave in almost immediately. I took one of the loaves, vaguely hoping they hadn't been counted, and fled with my plunder.

I ate the bread—a mixture of rye and bran—in secret, voluptuously, strolling along the empty alleys of the camp, packing my stomach with this stodgy mass. It must have weighed a couple of pounds, and within ten minutes I managed to swallow three-quarters of it before stalling. Then, like the chump I was, I hid the rest under my mattress to have it with our evening soup.

Within the hour, I found myself nose to nose with the dwarf. He gave me a piercing look, and I could instantly tell that, in spite of my efforts to look innocent, he knew, and I was in for it.

"Junge, du hast ein Brot gestohlen. Wo ist dein Bett?" Kid, you stole a loaf. Where's your bed?

He lifted up the mattress, revealing the remains of the corpus delicti, and gave me a good thrashing. When he'd finished, all I could say was, *"Ich habe es verdient."* I deserved it.

He had the right to kill me. He'd killed others for less.

He finally decided I would replace the bread out of my weekly rations, and the matter would end there. Then he said to me, "You idiot, why didn't you tell me you were hungry?" (He used the word *Kohldampf,* "cabbage steam," which meant "hunger" in camp slang.) "I would have given you some food."

As if it were possible not to be hungry!

The incident ended our relationship. Stealing bread was considered a serious crime. I lost the many privileges I'd enjoyed thanks to my strange protector.

It took me almost a year to prove to him that I was capable of surviving and that although I couldn't live in the camp as he did, like a fish in water, I was at least able to make a place for myself there. We wound up becoming good friends again, and I can easily imagine that if any common criminal survived Auschwitz, it was he.

Around 1960, while in Hamburg on business, I was riding in a taxi near the Reeperbahn, the city's red-light district, when I thought I glimpsed the dwarf in the neon light of a facade; perhaps he'd gone back to his former profession, pimping . . . The traffic was heavy. There was no way the taxi could have stopped.

At the end of roll call a week after registration, we found out our assignments. Block number, *Kommando* number. We were out of quarantine and had become, all too often temporarily, active members of the community.

The *Kommando* of chemists had not yet been set up, since the factory wasn't operational. I was in Block 26, Philippe in Block 24. Both of us were in *Kommando* 3: heavy work of various kinds, one of the most undesirable labor gangs, a great consumer of men. There were almost a hundred of us. Then came weeks of horror: reveille at 5:30, roll call, departure with the *Kommando* after the morning's bread, marching to the music of the band as the work details headed out, in step, in rows of five. Arriving at the factory, we'd be set to unloading wagons, or digging trenches, or laying pipes, or stacking bricks.

How can I explain the threat posed by two bricks, two of those bricks clapped together that one sees flying from hand to hand among a team of masons? They seem to possess a life of their own, like a basketball. They hardly touch those bare hands, seem to take on a spurt of energy and continue on to their destination, where they're piled one upon the other. A graceful curve, uninterrupted, accompanied by the laughter and traditional songs of those proverbially merry tradesmen.

Those same bricks that are thrown at me by a lawyer, who received them from a Latin teacher, who got them from a furrier. Our hands are sheathed in huge, torn mittens. The bricks never arrive at the same angle, or the same speed, or the same place; sometimes the pair separates along the way. When they land on the ground in front of you, you get beaten. Insults don't count. They come from the civilian foreman; the blows are from the *Kapo*. Good luck if there's an SS man around! Then it's kicks, and the whip.

Usually, of course, it's the bad thrower who's at fault, in the end. A morning lasts a long time, scores even out. Sometimes the bricks just can't be caught and you get hell, sometimes you throw any which way and the other guy gets it.

Our hands, used to holding newspapers, pens, forks, perhaps briefcases, turn out to be incompetent, some more than others.

And so there are hopeless cases, with bleeding hands, who will never learn. The bricks fall on their feet. The blows fall on their heads. Here, an open wound doesn't scab over. For them, the writing is on the wall. The bricks are killers.

As for me, I must have been slightly above average. Not much technique but a good eye, and I'd played some basketball. Even so, my hands were flayed raw, and just below the index finger of my right hand I developed a small, pus-filled crater. I'm looking at the oval scar as I write these lines.

Return at 5:00 P.M. Roll call, back to the block, a liter of evening soup. I saw Philippe melting away like an ice cube before my eyes. And I who had been a chubby adolescent, whose graceful shots at the basket had earned me the less-than-flattering nickname "the Elegant Elephant" at Claude-Bernard—I, too, felt my strength and stamina ebbing fast. In the early days, Philippe and I somehow found the will to see each other for a moment after supper, before collapsing on our straw bedding like farm animals.

Coming back to the camp one afternoon, I fell at the worst moment, when the *Kommando* filed by the SS, eyes right. The *Kapo* was announcing the number of the squad and personnel: "*Kommando 3, 85 Männer.*" I received a barrage of kicks that opened up my right leg. The wounds later became ulcers that would plague me until the spring of 1946, one year after my return to France. Philippe helped me up and walked me back to my block.

I had the wounds dressed in the KB, the infirmary. Seeing me there, Waitz shook his head: I was off to a bad start. Feldbaum slathered me with his grotesque ointments. One, a black, smelly lotion called Ichytol, cleaned out cuts, while another salve, of a lovely orange color, was popular because it was greasy and kept sores warm. Full of good intentions, Feldbaum automatically advised me to take it easy on my leg, then realized what he'd just said and flashed me a big (if slightly embarrassed) smile: "Come back if it gets worse, I'll try to have you hospitalized for a day or two."

The next morning, I set out as best I could for work. I spent an hour or so ensconced in the latrines, sitting down, nice and warm, with the blessing of a *Kapo* who was almost human. Now and then a colleague would come sit on the convivial bench and give free rein to his chronic diarrhea. We'd exchange a few gloomy remarks. He'd catch his breath, pull up his pants, and slog back to his shovel or his bricks.

Returning to camp at dusk, I was limping so badly I had trouble keeping up. As we reached the main gate, for the regulation march-past, I made a supreme effort. The senior camp inmate was watching our arrival. He caught sight of me and saw, with a practiced eye, that I'd hit bottom. He pulled me from the ranks.

"Junge," he said, "this *Kommando* is too hard for you. Come see me tonight."

He had a tidy house, almost a villa, in the middle of the camp, where he royally entertained a few lordly veterans in the evenings. He probably lived better there than he had on the outside.

Physically, he was imposing, a hulk, a brute force, and his voice, a bass à la Chaliapin, boomed out effortlessly over any surrounding noise. He enjoyed the privilege of not having his head shaved. Some said he'd been a bank robber and had killed a few *Schupos*, uniformed policemen. Others claimed he'd been a gang boss and neighborhood racketeer, like in Chicago.

The SS had picked a good one: he was a wild animal, an exterminator, the perfect henchman to carry out their plans. He worked with a pick, with a blackjack, with a nail-studded club, with his bare hands, with booted kicks, on his own initiative, according to his mood, without hatred, as a seasoned professional criminal.

He had his moments of good humor, as when we'd first met, and of satisfaction in keeping a human being alive, just for fun or as a challenge. I think he was lucid enough, in his morbid madness, to know that his life would soon be cut short. He lugged around a sort of cold fury, perhaps in the end a kind of despair that gave him a certain magnetism, the aura of a monster.

I knocked on his door, which opened. He was surrounded by his usual court: the heads of the labor records and camp maintenance offices, two or three senior block inmates. I looked around, somewhat dazed. It was a real room, full of *Gemütlichkeit,* with white curtains at the windows, an oilcloth on the rectangular table, and what looked like the remains of a meal, a genuine meal, solid food eaten with a knife and fork.

I have the vague impression—or would it be a trick of the imagination? But no, an image is forming—that there were two pots of withered flowers on the inside windowsills. The master of the house did not have a green thumb. A drawn curtain in the back probably concealed a shower and perhaps even, why not, a proper toilet.

Meanwhile, I had limped the three steps separating me from the *Lagerältester,* whom I greeted with all the outward signs of respect due his position.

He commented on my case: "*Ein kleiner Franzose,* a French kid, but he speaks three languages, and he's a chemist. In *Kommando* 3, he won't make it."

Turning to the head of the labor records office, he said, "Tomorrow, you'll put him in a nice safe *Kommando* . . . Show us your leg," he ordered me. I lifted up my pant leg, revealing the bloodied paper bandages. "Now go to bed," he said, "and get yourself a liter of soup on the way, from Willi." Willi was his factotum. I didn't need to be told twice. I headed for the door. He called me back. "*Junge,* watch out for the block bosses and the *Kapos.*" Then he winked and added, "Don't get too close."

I'd already wised up a little, and although I wasn't exactly sure what he was getting at, I had a vague idea.

I was to learn rather quickly later on that, like a young lady of good family fresh from the Convent of Innocent Young Things, I'd have to defend my virtue fiercely. Not to comply with any supposed morality—I had no more inhibitions on that score and in extreme necessity would certainly have given in—but because the potential implications were stamped "immediate and mortal danger."

As for the senior camp inmate and a few other hierarchs, they enjoyed the pleasures of a mobile bordello that visited our premises once a month on its tour to service the executioners. Perhaps somewhere in the Parisian neighborhood of Passy, on Vienna's Ringstrasse, in the beautiful Berlin suburb of Wannsee, or in the ancient Hungarian city of Pest, there still lives an old lady who weathered that particular experience.

The next morning I was transferred to *Kommando* 12, assigned to clean up an underground warehouse where chemical products were to be stored. We spent the day leaning on our brooms, which we set in motion when anyone came to check on us.

At noon, our *Kapo* organized—that was the time-honored term for obtaining food or other necessities illegally through theft, barter, or the black market—a double ration of soup. Naturally it was hot water seasoned with a few nutritive remnants, since I. G. Farben was not partial to unprofitable investments, but it warmed us up. As for Philippe, he hadn't had my luck. I'd been able to take him only the liter of soup given me by the *Lagerältester*.

As the days went by and exhaustion set in, we saw each other only at roll call. Neither of us had the strength to cross the camp to visit the other, unless it was a holiday Sunday.

One morning in late November I vomited my bread. Pissing in the snow, I saw my urine was a dark ocher. A German doctor in a neighboring bunk looked at my eyes and proclaimed me jaundiced. "Lucky stiff," he told me, "they'll put you in the KB." I dragged myself to the infirmary, where a hundred raging optimists came daily to complain of dysentery, heart attacks, respiratory problems—and were sent back to work (save for the spectacular exception) with a few cheery words and some pixie dust.

I was one of the day's exceptions. They sent me to the contagious-diseases ward. I stripped off my clothes, keeping only a shirt, and, thanking my lucky stars, lay down among the tubercular, the typhus-racked, and my comrades in hepatitis.

Thus passed two or three weeks that have left not a single trace in my memory. This punishing and untreatable illness left me drained and probably just about done for.

At some point I was told that my brother—what brother? Philippe? Oh yes, Philippe—was in a bed in the next room. I toyed with the idea of getting up to go see my friend. I didn't have the courage. Five or six days later, I had by some miracle taken a turn for the better. I asked the doctor where Philippe was and what was wrong with him.

"Philippe?" he replied. "But he died three days ago. He emptied out and passed away."

In this chapter I have written about our shared collapse and the death of Philippe. My friend. For whom I felt an infinite tenderness, which he returned. And before I bring this chapter to a close, I have to say that I've done my very best to remember what he looked like, his face, his profile, the sound of his voice. I've tried to pull him out of my memory with forceps.

There's nothing left, not the slightest trace. If I went back fifty years, would I even recognize him?

Philippe died. And now he has died again, forever. Am I not the last being on this earth to have known him when he was alive and to have loved him, before letting him leave without holding his hand?

The week I returned to Paris, I telephoned *L'Aurore*. I left a message for M. Hagenauer, which said explicitly that I had some bad news for him. I don't know exactly what was in the message he received; perhaps they didn't want to crush his hopes completely.

He showed up all out of breath that very evening. I asked him to sit down and informed him his son was dead. Not brutally, of course; I told him our story, spoke about the friendship we had shared, and our common suffering, and the precious aid and support he had brought me.

I spoke the last word of my last sentence. My hair was still stubble, my cheeks sunken; he looked at me for a few seconds, began to cry, and ran away.

I never saw him again.

Digression II

It's already a month since I began writing, and I'm starting to feel the effects of my plunge into the depths. My sleep grows more and more troubled. As I lie awake at night for hours, my disconnected brain dredges up images I thought were dead and buried. That's how the faces of Dr. Ohrenstein and others have come back to life. My memory is sweating, oozing.

I spend almost every hour of the day and night diving away, to such an extent that a weekend trip with my wife, Simone—to Bruges for the Hans Memling retrospective, then on to Ghent to see *The Mystic Lamb* again—was not as enjoyable as I'd expected. I missed my sheets of white paper. My mind doesn't wander anymore: as soon as I set it free, it gets right down to business, counting sacrificial sheep.

Roger and Nicole came for the weekend; other friends have been over for dinner on a few occasions. I'm quite capable of taking part in conversations, but inevitably, sooner or later, and almost unconsciously, I return to my puzzle. I say things. They exchange glances . . .

As my writing has taken shape, I've run into a major problem I had not anticipated. I'm having difficulty separating two time frames: the description of the event as it happened (or at least as I remember it) and the vision or interpretation of it I tend to favor after later experience has erased the initial impression.

The gaping holes where nothing concrete remains of weeks or even months of bodily misery will force me to tax my imagination in this reconstruction. Still, I do have landmarks I can rely on. I ought to be able to get very close to what really happened. Absolute paradox: speaking of reality in relation to that universe . . .

I must not let the writings of other witnesses affect me.

I'm now certain of what I want to avoid: the museum of horrors, the litany of atrocities. Everything has been said, sometimes too cruelly.

I don't wish to offer up a picture of daily life, either, except indirectly. And even if I wanted to, I'd be hard-pressed; after fifty years, memory is more fragile than moth-eaten lace. What I do want is enormously ambitious, perhaps—and therefore hardly practical.

To portray anguish. A world where you sink because you don't know how to swim.

To follow the process, the degradation of human beings before annihilation. The death of feeling, the death of thought, then the death of the man.

To show the curve dropping to zero. The point of no return.

Then, for a lucky few of us, gradual adaptation, the upward climb, and transformation into a different variety of human being, no longer *Homo sapiens* but "extermination-camp man."

A species whose life span proved fleeting. Two or three years. As opposed to the Neanderthals' thirty thousand or the one hundred and fifty thousand of *Homo habilis*. But a species with much to teach the sociologists of the future.

Oddly enough, I'm not in any distress. Even better, I'm experiencing a kind of sensual pleasure: I'm purging myself as I write, and I have a vague feeling not of liberation, but of fulfilled obligation.

A strange vacation assignment, one I've been planning for fifty years, for the moment in my life when I could freely devote myself to it. After my working days are over, before decrepitude sets in . . .

The Black Hole

According to Waitz, it seems I'm the exception that proves the rule: I'll survive my hepatitis. Philippe is dead, and we're in January. Through the windows of the isolation ward I see the snowy courtyard and the furtive shadows of poor frozen zebras trying to escape the biting cold. I count the days left to go: ten in January, all of February, and even the first half of March. Every day spent in the infirmary is a small victory. The accumulation of victories means survival and the arrival of spring.

No dream lasts forever: they finally tell me they can't keep me any longer. I must return to the block, the roll calls, the *Kommando*. The doctors have gone to the absolute limit of their authority. I'm fortunate, I'm among those they try to help survive, one for every ten they must abandon to their fates.

On the appointed day, I leave my sickbed behind and return to the fray. Storeroom clerk: this time around, I get pathetic rags and clogs that weigh a ton. Barber: my head is shaved bald once again.

Bath in a tub with disinfectants that burn my leg. A farewell bandage. Feldbaum pats my hand and tells me not to lose heart.

I step out of the infirmary. The cold grabs my throat like a wolf—I've been living in an overheated room for more than a month. Luckily, thanks to the *Lagerältester,* I'm reassigned to my original block and *Kommando.* There's probably a cross on my registration card in the office, indicating that I'm a more or less privileged inmate.

Your basic *Häftling* is here today, gone tomorrow, packed off wherever he is needed, and he is needed, as a rule, by the *Kommandos* that spare no one.

I get to the block and present my card to the *Stubendienst,* who recognizes me. He assigns me to a top bunk, which I'll be sharing. The block is overcrowded. We'll be sleeping top-to-tail, the head of one bedfellow at the other's feet. I have the rest of the day to prepare to go back on the chain gang.

The *Kommandos* return, the band plays its usual cheery tunes. Souza marches . . . The tunes that still make me grit my teeth when I hear them at a beach resort's bandstand or on some tiresome provincial radio station.

The evening roll call lasts more than an hour. I'd had enough time to find a string to use as a belt, and even a greasy piece of wrapping paper to slip beneath my shirt. Standing still in the cold is a torment I'd almost forgotten. Yet before I'd fallen ill, we'd already had roll calls of two or three hours in temperatures ten degrees below freezing.

At last the signal to disperse lets us return to our barracks. The evening soup will be distributed. We line up. You have to time things just right to get your turn when the soup's low in the pot, thick with little chunks of potato. I don't care about this anymore. My incompletely cured hepatitis leaves me nauseated, without appetite. I have to force myself to swallow my clear soup and by an irony of fate, when the *Stubendienst* who'd seen me that morning calls me over for a second ladleful, my first impulse is to refuse, to say, "No thanks." Then, realizing I'd cause a scandal by creating a situation unheard of in the whole history of the camp, I go get the second helping and offer it to my nearest pal. He obviously doesn't believe his eyes and cannot understand that I'm compelled to be his benefactor.

I go to bed for a night that is dreamless, too brief, and haunted by dread of the next day.

I wrote "dreamless" almost automatically, without thinking. I suddenly realize that I don't ever remember talking or hearing about dreams, except perhaps in the infirmary, toward the end of my illness.

I'm not even talking about erotic dreams, which were psychologically and physiologically beyond us, but those dreams you have in the early morning, which you remember after awaking and talk over with your friends. Those dreams of escape into another reality, harmless, sometimes foolish flights of fancy.

Our sleep is interrupted by the need to piss; by the sporadic movements of our bunkmates, lying head to toe, whose feet are wriggling on the straw pillow; by the snoring of two hundred block inmates, the moans of the injured, the rounds of the *Stubendienst* . . . Our slumbers are disturbed a hundred times for a fraction of a second, before we sink back into an almost cataleptic lethargy prescribed, no doubt, by our frantic desire to survive.

Perhaps dreams are a luxury? A waste of vital energy? Will some scientist, a sleep specialist, look into this matter one day and come up with a few answers?

Maybe the lack of dreams even helps explain the madness of the veteran apparatchiks who mistreat us, when they're not killing us.

At 5:30 A.M., the fateful cry that means the day's tribulations have begun: *"Aufstehen!"* Get up! Brief wash for those who still care about cleanliness. Distribution of bread along with the pat of margarine, slice of sausage, or piece of cheese. It's double rations this morning and by general agreement the least awful moment of the day. Barely able to get down a single ration, I keep the rest for noon at the factory.

Everyone savors the bread. In a solemn silence, each person takes care not to drop one crumb. The spoon handles, patiently sharpened, cut into the bread, spread the margarine, slice the sausage in two. We chew slowly, to extract the goodness and facilitate digestion. An hour's free time when those fallen ill overnight can try their chances at the infirmary. Finally, morning roll call, a brief one so as not to delay departure to the factory.

I. G. Farben pays the SS a daily flat rate per slave laborer.

Under the direction of an Austrian conductor, the band (which Robert Frances, a talented flutist, had been unable to join for lack of breath) accompanies the departing procession of *Kommandos*.

We walk toward Buna in ranks of five, dragging our clogs in the mud or snow, carrying our bowls for the noon soup clamped under our arms. It's raining. An icy rain with gusts of wind that have the run of this flat, dreary plain in Silesia.

The *Kommando* is one of the benign sort. Cleaning, readying materials for heavy labor, stacking bricks at the very worst. It's still too much.

After ten o'clock, you have to husband your energy every minute. A moment lingering near a brazier. A trip to the latrines, which doesn't need to be faked: almost all of us are suffering from larval dysentery. The *Kapo* usually turns a blind eye. Every now and then the arrival of a *Meister*—a German foreman—or even an SS officer provokes a spasm of feverish activity, urged on by the theatrical shouts of the *Kapo*. When the bad moment has passed we catch our breath. Brief pause at noon, when the siren blows.

The German and Polish workers and foremen, the volunteer workers, the prisoners of war, the forced laborers—the whole scurrying mass collected from the four points of the compass to feed the German industrial machine—now gets out its lunch.

I can still see the Polish workmen unwrapping their country bread and bacon. They cut cubes of both with knives, stuff in huge mouthfuls, chew noisily. The eyes of poor starving devils follow their every move. They cannot be unaware of this. They pretend. To them, we don't exist. We don't belong to the same species. We're the inmates of a zoo where it's forbidden to feed the animals.

We, the pariahs of this caste society, we wait for our miserable pittance, which some of us supplement with a slice of bread saved from the morning's ration.

All this is normal, no one acts surprised. Occasionally, rarely, you hear about a gesture of compassion. Times are hard, each community keeps to itself.

Back to work: we still have three and a half hours to go. Two hundred and ten minutes that crawl by slowly, so slowly. The blessed days when we work indoors are vacations we enjoy to the fullest. Other times, you have to try getting a turn at slipping into the tool shed, where the *Kapo* takes shelter.

Darkness falls early, around four o'clock. The cold becomes more gripping, especially since hunger and fatigue are taking their toll.

At last comes the signal for *Feierabend,* time to knock off work. The factory empties out, the *Kommandos* form up and begin the walk back. The prospect of hot soup and sleep, after the trial of the evening roll call, gives even the weakest among us some strength.

The brief period when I came the closest to my own death—overwhelmed by chronic dysentery, enfeebled by the hepatitis of which I think I was the sole survivor—still haunts me like a nightmare.

I caught scabies from my bunkmate. The itching began between my fingers, then gradually invaded my entire body. At night, dead to the world, I would scratch myself bloody without realizing it, and in the early morning, when we heard the sinister sound of reveille, I'd get up staggering with fatigue.

Treatment for scabies was administered every evening. You had to wait in line in front of the *Krankenbau,* out in the cold, with a hundred other scabby sufferers. They'd smear our bodies with a revolting liquid stinking strongly of sulfur. Then I'd go get a fresh bandage on my ulcers, which were slowly getting bigger.

I must have reached the same point as Philippe, before his hospitalization and death. I could see reflected in other people's eyes the image of a *Muselmann* in the making. A *Muselmann* whose time was running out. Me.

I had become obsessed with the cold. I tried every trick in the book to escape it, at the risk of being beaten. At evening roll call, the suffering became palpable, something biting to the bone, screamingly painful. I thought I would never ever get warm again.

Dysentery put the final touch to my degradation. How many times, during the six weeks in January and February I spent on that *Kommando,* did I cover the last mile back to camp with my right hand jammed between my buttocks to keep the diarrhea that was slowly draining me from soaking through my trousers and running down my legs into my clogs? At the camp entrance, you had to march in time with the band, eyes right and sphincter tight. Hundreds of us walked with that telltale step. Fodder for the next selection.

The ability to fart loudly is the prime outward sign of health that distinguishes a camp aristocrat, who exercises this privilege to the point of petomania. It's the test of nonliquidity. When a newcomer in our midst—or one of us between bouts of diarrhea—decides to let out a blast, he earns the compliments and envy of all around him, who continue to clench their cheeks.

At the KB they are quite helpless to combat this diarrhea, which is the combined result of physical debilitation, contaminated water, soups made from turnips, beets, and cabbage. Your poor average *Häftling* is treated with an absurd product baptized *Bolus alba,* which is nothing but a kind of pasty white plaster that is supposed to cement up our bowels and that no one can swallow without gagging.

That's why you see human ruins here and there in the camp with the white-painted mouths of clowns. Feldbaum usually manages to slip me a few pills of Tannalbin, which I suppose is an albumin compound. It plugs up my digestive system for twenty-four hours and gives me a painfully bloated belly. On the other hand, I can walk around without leaking.

We've become experts in comparative entomology, with particular competence in the carnivorous species: fleas, lice, and bedbugs.

Lice are the most dangerous because they carry typhus. There's an inspection in the block twice a week. You have to show your shirt—or what passes for it—to a "specialized" *Stubendienst,* who examines the seams and folds where the tiny creatures live. Inmates with lice are sent immediately to be disinfected.

The bedbugs are the most ferocious. Their bites itch for hours. As for the fleas, they're our ladies in waiting, hopping from one to another of us when the blood on offer begins to run dry.

Luckily for me, I can ignore the distractions afforded us by these domestic vermin. Scabies requires my full and constant attention. Not until I'm cured of that will I learn to distinguish bedbugs from fleas.

Of those weeks I remember only wretchedness, cold, and humiliation. And what about human relations? They don't exist. I'm surrounded by filmy wraiths I can barely see, who evaporate as the days go by. This one's hospitalized, he'll die for sure. That one's selected for the gas chamber. Here are three new faces, Italians, it seems. They'll burn out quickly, if you'll pardon the expression.

I've withdrawn inside my shell: all the vital energy I have left is mobilized for my own survival.

My bunkmate remains anonymous to me; his feet have a particular, pungent odor, the only tie between us, other than scabies. Death feels peckish and pops him down the hatch. In exchange I get a Greek from Salonika, one of those the camp has unflatteringly nicknamed "Klepsi-klepsies"; the handful that remain of them are rumored to be indestructible.

This one is sociable and easy to get along with. He doesn't steal anything from me and even worries about my injured leg, which he avoids bumping when he climbs down to piss at night. We sleep like the dead.

All the human beings around me are interchangeable: the one who rubs my back on roll call square, the one who walks beside me to the work site at Buna, the one in front of me in line for our evening soup.

Here today, gone tomorrow. Eeny, meeny, miney, moe.

The happy-go-lucky gang we formed in Drancy—I count off the deaths like daisy petals, without batting an eye. My last feelings died out with Philippe.

Our flesh and muscles melt away, our teeth loosen, our guts liquefy, our wounds fester, and we die, we die, we die.

Perchance a deus ex machina—an SS officer, a *Kapo,* a block boss—precipitates the finale with a bullet, a pickax blow, a clubbing. Sometimes, more rarely, one of us is saved from our common grave by him the way an oil-soaked penguin or seal will be picked out, years later, for washing, nursing, feeding, to see if it recuperates and survives.

And I take this absurd, mephitic universe for granted, as though nothing else had ever existed. I have no feelings of anguish, no more than I have questions. It all goes without saying. I'm at the age where one adjusts, and I economize on everything by getting rid of moral suffering, emotions, memories—and regrets as well, a crucial imperative. It's wasteful to give your affection to ghosts on reprieve. Why set yourself up for tears the next day? The time will perhaps come, if I live, when I'll be able to love again, unless I've become sterile.

Strangely enough, it seems to me that I've never envisaged my death except abstractly. Someone once said that what you cannot imagine has no existence. Maybe I had stumbled on the recipe for immortality.

Well, one morning I woke up with a raging fever. I managed to get myself to the infirmary. Ohrenstein looked at my cheek and diagnosed erysipelas, a disease peculiar to pigs and the occasional human. He hospitalized me straightaway.

Through some miracle Feldbaum came up with two doses of Prontosil, a recently discovered sulfa drug, effective against streptococci. I swallowed twelve dark red pills in two batches and I emerged from my delirium to find myself safe and warm. I was going to make it to spring.

The Last Salon

The sulfa drug bested my erysipelas, leaving my doctor pals looking at number 157,239 reduced to a pre-*Muselmann* state by the parade of hepatitis, dysentery, and infectious diseases, and what's more, suffering from a leg covered with sores.

We were coming up on four months since they had seen me land in the camp and decided to take a chance on me, without my knowledge. I'd certainly set off on the wrong foot.

I've often thought about this problem of choice that constantly confronted them. It was impossible for the doctors to save or even help everyone. What criteria did they use? The anonymous *Häftling* was programmed to last two months, three if he was exceptionally strong and arrived in good shape. Were their choices dictated by age, nationality, education, physical beauty, social status, profession, or sympathy? They who had taken the Hippocratic oath, how did they feel about rejecting the others? After the war, Waitz returned to his professorship in medicine at the University of Strasbourg. I think the questions he must have asked himself became almost an obsession. You can't argue with material impossibility. But it neither consoles you nor lets you off the hook.

The doctors let some die to save others. I saw people around me die, but I was saved. That was enough to make me feel uneasy, guilty of being too lucky, of having left the others to their common fate. Of course, these feelings surfaced later, after my rebirth. They stemmed from a morality that had become obsolete in the camp.

Sometimes I imagine that Waitz, Ohrenstein, Feldbaum, and the others discussed my case, wondering if I was still able to recover. Or maybe they did nothing of the sort and simply carried me as far along as they could.

At any rate, with luck on my side, I repaid their efforts, and they won their wager.

They decided to stash me safely in the *Schonungsblock* for a few weeks, long enough for me to weather the winter.

Schonung: "care," the convalescents' block. The height of irrationality in this anti-Cartesian universe par excellence, the world of the concentration camp. I don't know if there was a *Schonungsblock* anywhere else besides Monowitz. A sumptuous aberration.

Whereas the system runs on manpower worked to the point of collapse or death and replaced through new arrivals, abundantly available, here is a place provided for the care of convalescents, of those not seriously ill, that operates under the pretext of getting them back on their feet and that in reality offers them a place of shelter. The doctors are the ones who set up this small island of peace. But with the permission and under the supervision of an SS doctor. The condition imposed in return is a monthly selection.

So once a month an SS commission inspects the inmates of the block and picks some of them out, the decisive factor being the lack of buttocks, the last reservoir of vital energy.

The inspection takes place as a march-past on the double, shirts hiked up, in front of the comfortably seated SS. The head block physician marks on his list the numbers indicated by the commission. More than once, he takes the risk of skipping a number or two. Perhaps I was even spared by such a gesture?

Those selected are told they will be transferred to the main infirmary in Auschwitz I. Some believe this. I happen to know that they have between six and twelve hours left to live and that what's in store for them is Zyklon B.

One fine morning I move from the contagious ward to Bora Bora.

The *Schonungsblock* lies between the infirmary and the camp. It's a classic block, four rows of three-tiered bunks, three aisles, and in the front, the room for the *Stubendienst* and the head block physician, who is none other than the good Dr. Ohrenstein.

Ohrenstein is a Rumanian Jewish doctor who settled in France in 1930. A general practitioner, he had an office in the neighborhood of Les Halles. He had been on the same transport as I was. I've rarely seen a fellow so overflowing with human warmth. Among the handful of survivors, there isn't one who doesn't cherish his memory, from having received of him whatever he had to give. I know nothing of how he died during the evacuation. Sometimes I tell myself that if I had been there, I would have helped him—forced him—to live. He is with me still.

·   ·   ·

I snagged an upper bunk and met my fellow convalescents. The corner where I set up housekeeping was a little France.

All through that month of February 1944, I lived in this miraculous oasis a civilized, social, educational life that today seems to me completely unreal, given the schizophrenic world that was slowly consuming us.

The only hitch: hunger, sharpened by idleness. I endured it better than the others, not burning much in the way of energy. I was coming out ahead on my caloric intake.

And so, I made friends fairly quickly with a small group of my companions in good fortune.

When we awoke in the morning, the *Kommandos* were already out in the snow and the killing cold, slogging off to Buna. We would collect our ration of bread with its trimmings, along with a hot drink pompously referred to as tea. After wishing one another good morning and sharing a bit of small talk, followed by a brief toilette, we'd settle down to enjoy this breakfast.

A full belly promotes napping, so we'd stretch the night out until about noon.

The afternoon would find us alert, in good spirits, and what's more, stimulated by our growing hunger and anticipation of the evening soup.

Then the little circle we had formed would gather, and discussions would begin.

Jean Olchanski was from the upper middle class, the manager of a company, a person of dazzling culture and education in my schoolboy's eyes. In spite of the patched shirt that served as his bathrobe and revealed his behind whenever he had to climb down from his bunk, he seemed supremely distinguished to me. I found it hard to use the familiar *tu* with him. Although he behaved in a paternal way toward me, he treated me as an adult, which was flattering. It was a kind of relationship I hadn't known in my former life.

I remember that one day, speaking about a possible future in which I would find no trace left of my family, he offered to adopt me.

Robert Frances had been reading for his university teaching exam in philosophy; he was six or seven years older than I was, while Olchanski was in his forties. To me Robert had all the prestige of a university man, of the professor he seemed destined to become. He gave the impression of great gentleness, and fragility. He was a musician as well, not only a flutist but a composer and pianist. I drank in his words. I was at an age when one needs an intellectual mentor. I had found mine.

Sometimes I told myself that this fount of culture would soon dry up, that I should listen, and remember. I never imagined that Robert might survive, as he could play none of the trump cards that made it possible to hope. Neither a profession that might be turned to some use, nor sufficient knowledge of German, nor any privileged connections to exploit.

The third of our number was a young actor. His stage name was Jacques Dasque or something like that. He had been operated on for a phlegmon, an ulcerative inflammation, and through I don't know what medical slipup, while he was under the anesthetic, scalding hot-water bottles had been placed beneath his feet. He had third-degree burns on his heels and thick paper bandages swaddling his feet, which were slathered with smelly ointment. He must have been Robert's age, and he recited poetry to us. He knew—among other things—all of Verlaine by heart, and when he recited,

Je suis venu pauvre orphelin,
Riche de mes seuls yeux tranquilles,
Vers les hommes des grandes villes,
Ils ne m'ont pas trouvé malin.

Forth I came, a poor orphan,
Rich only in my candid gaze,
To meet the townfolk of my days,
Who did not find me a clever man.

I was sorry I had no more tears to shed.

Instead of healing, his feet had become infected. I took him for lost, and he was. Shortly after I left the block, a selection sealed his fate. I don't think he knew what was waiting for him.

As luck would have it, Jean and Robert are still alive. Jean managed to escape during the evacuation. He hid in a barn in Gleiwitz for ten days, stealing food at night from an abandoned farm. He held out that way until the Russians arrived, then crossed Poland and the Ukraine to finally reach Odessa. He was repatriated two months after the war ended.

As for Robert, defying all the statistical odds, he made it to the evacuation. From Gleiwitz he plunged into a hellish journey, a guided tour of the best camps still available during that off-season, and wound up on a road in Bavaria with a small group of other miraculous survivors. The SS, contrary to their custom, abandoned them alive. All they had to do was wait for the Americans.

The previous day, Feldbaum the athlete, Feldbaum who had nursed us all in the infirmary, Feldbaum had died, by the side of the road, like a run-over dog.

Since I'd remembered Robert's address, I contacted his sister when I got back to Paris. I told her that on the eighteenth of January I had seen him alive and that he had a reasonable chance of making it. The following week, he came home.

Forty years later, he wrote a book, *Intact aux yeux du monde* (*Whole in the Eyes of the World*), which allowed me to find him again. The first thing he said when he came to see me was, "We beat them."

Who will tell me through what alchemy Robert the Reed survived without anyone's help and Feldbaum the Oak, who had everything on his side, was destroyed? Death, where is thy logic?

Perhaps there is some mysterious gene that safeguards those who have it, a gene that staves off death to the very last possible moment. A gene that makes you allergic to death.

Every once in a while, our little discussion group would be joined by Dr. Freze. He was an older man of almost sixty, who had probably slipped through thanks to a moment's distraction on the part of his colleague, Dr. Mengele. He couldn't join the medical personnel of the KB because he didn't know a word of German. A few days on a *Kommando* had been enough to put him out of commission, and it was decided to find a spot for him in the *Schonungsblock* as a night guard. He suffered from serious edema, among other things, which swelled his legs to elephantine size, and I can still see him pressing his bunched fingers into the flesh to watch the livid hollow slowly fill in again.

His Midi accent was so broad it sounded fake. He had wandered right out of a Pagnol novel and into our midst.

His duties consisted of supervising the tub used as a portable toilet, which enjoyed the constant attentions of the soup-pissers and dysentery-dribblers—in short, the population of the entire block. When the tub was brimful, it was Dr. Freze's job to mobilize the last customer, who would help him lug it with two stretcher poles to the cesspit for emptying.

I volunteered more than once to give him a hand. Now that we were no longer physically exhausted, we'd all become lighter sleepers. I would put on wooden clogs. We'd pick up the tub with our poles fitted into two handles on the sides and set off through the snow, trying to avoid splashing. We'd empty the contents with the same well-synchronized movements and return to the block, where four or five habitués would be awaiting our return with legitimate impatience, buttocks clenched. Then I would sit down beside him, and we'd chat.

Sometimes he would talk about recipes and especially about the sublime bouillabaisses he'd feasted on in those far-off days when he was the mayor of Sainte-Maxime. He maintained that conger eel, hogfish, and rockfish were essential to a successful bouillabaisse, that adding burbot was a heresy, and that those who went so far as to mention a spiny lobster deserved to be hanged by the neck until dead. I learned everything about the preparation of rouille, the better olive oils, and the comparative merits of Parmesan and Gruyère on the side. He spoke to me as well about the scents of spring, of mimosas and parasol pines.

At daybreak, he would go to bed and sleep straight through until midafternoon, then rejoin us. That's how he lived, faultlessly carrying out his assignment, until January. He was among those who, like Primo Levi, remained in the camp, for he could hardly have managed to walk even half a mile. After ten days of famine and suspense, with people dying all around him, he saw the Russian vanguard arrive. He returned home, was triumphantly reelected mayor, and lived happily to the end of his days. A street in Sainte-Maxime today bears his name.

Early every afternoon, our little Areopagus would begin its cultural activities. I thus witnessed a collaboration between Robert and Jean to reconstruct the three movements of the Symphony in D Minor by César Franck, whose name was new to me. One would whistle a theme, the other would join in, adding counterpoint, and little by little the symphony became familiar to me. Six weeks after my return, the first public concert I ever attended was conducted one Sunday by Tony Aubin, leading the Pasdeloup Orchestra in the Salle Pleyel. The main offering on the program was the Symphony in D Minor.

It was also my first classical record.

There were philosophical debates involving the ancient Greeks, Kant, Kierkegaard. They analyzed the *Critique of Pure Reason,* which I remembered when I later read Louis Guilloux's novel about World War I, *Le Sang Noir (Black Blood).**

In my ignorance, I had to listen silently to all these discussions. The best I could do was venture a question when I was seriously lost, and most of it went right over my head.

Once in a while, we'd talk about literature. There I was knowledgeable beyond my years. I'd read a lot, especially foreign works, Russian, English, American authors, while my friends' expertise was rather typical: they were familiar with the most minor Renaissance poet of the Pléiade, the worst text by Lesage, the florid sermons of Cardinal de Bourdaloue, but they floundered a bit when I mentioned Oscar Wilde or Pushkin, let alone Mark Twain.

*Cripure—French university slang for Kant's *Critique de la raison pure*—is the name of a character in this savage tale.

Occasionally, tired of cultural conversations, particularly toward the end of the afternoon, when we were gnawed by hunger, we'd turn to Jean Olchanski, a discriminating gourmet, a frequenter of deluxe hotels and three-star restaurants.

He told us one day about a lunch in a restaurant that has long since vanished, the Relais de la Belle Aurore on place du Marché-Saint-Honoré. The specialty of the house was hors d'oeuvres, and he described for us the parade of some sixty little dishes. My mouth was watering so much I could hardly swallow fast enough. From crudités to foie gras, truffles to caviar, anchovies to shellfish, he conjured up temptations that would have overcome a saint. And we were patients in the *Schonungsblock* of Auschwitz III–Monowitz . . .

Another day, we learned all about the fine restaurants Androuet, Prunier on rue Duphot, and even Fernand Point's establishment in Vienne, just outside Lyon.

At the urging of Jacques, the actor, we made forays into the theater. He had been a pupil of Charles Dullin, the founder of the Théâtre de l'Atelier, and dreamed still of playing Shakespeare. He had played Cyrano de Bergerac on tour with Barret, and he performed the duel scene for us. I can see him now, straining forward on his bed, carefully protecting his mummified feet while he delivered the final verse: "At the end of the refrain, I strike home."

We did not overlook the fine arts. I still harbor from those days a particular fondness for the primitive Sienese painters so highly praised by Olchanski, for Piero della Francesca—the greatest of all, according to an occasional participant in our conversations, a patient whom I have completely forgotten . . . It's strange to think that this monthlong interlude has had such a decisive effect on my cultural interests and personal tastes.

. . .

Ohrenstein, the Doc, came by daily as though still doing rounds in a French hospital, but without an entourage of interns. He always lingered with us a little while, bringing us the latest news of the camp and the war.

One morning, he looked grim: there was to be a selection the next day. He told us that we were among the strongest patients, that there was no need to worry.

We experienced the humiliation of running in our shirts, chests thrust out, buttocks bared, in front of the SS doctors in uniform. Humiliation? Our dignity had already suffered much worse than that. We'd laughed about it among ourselves, it was no big deal. Our pride came back to us only much later, with the return of bread, knives and forks, and freedom.

Ten or twelve patients of our casual acquaintance freed up their beds and set out for a better world. We observed all this with the indifference to death that had become our common denominator.

Ever since then, I have been unable to behave with the proper respect, and compassion, and even presence one should show those who are dying. I have to force myself to express my sorrow to the bereaved. My own death is familiar to me, I know its face. I've glimpsed it often. Metaphysical anguish is as foreign to me as a distant galaxy. All this cuts me off from my fellow man.

That's how the month of February and the beginning of March went by. One after another, we all reached the end of our sick leave.

When I entered the *Schonungsblock,* I was at the lowest point of the sine curve describing my concentration camp experience, the point where, as a general rule, one threw in the towel. In the convalescent block I began the steady upward climb that in the end would save my life.

So I left our pleasant times behind, giving up culture and civilization, to confront the hell outside once more. Under normal temperature and pressure conditions, as chemists say.

One Sunday in Spring

Winter is behind us. I've survived, it's Napoleon's Austerlitz. The glorious, victorious sun of Austerlitz. What's more, it's Easter Sunday, a day off, and the weather is beautiful.

This dread of winter has dogged me all my life. I hate November, December, I wait impatiently for the days to grow longer and I know the calendar published by the postal service by heart: minus twenty-nine minutes of light in December, plus fifty-nine minutes in January. You don't gain the first minute in the morning until January 4. As soon as the thermometer dips below freezing, I get goosebumps and look for someone to rub my back. I defy anyone to be more allergic to winter sports than I am.

But as soon as the first stirrings of spring produce a bud on a precocious tree, I come back to life and I know that I've made it through the winter. Pavlov's conditioned reflex, Auschwitz III variant.

Feeling perkier after my stay in the *Schonungsblock,* I slowly regained strength and changed categories: from pre-*Muselmann* I became an acceptable *Häftling.* A relatively harmless *Kommando,*

pending the creation of the armada of chemists. A *Kapo* less ferocious than most, whom I learned to manage, more or less. A senior
block inmate who systematically favored the younger inmates, and
I was the youngest, which I lost no time in telling him, in my best
German.

A French forced laborer agreed to mail a letter for me, and, stu-
pefaction, six weeks later I received a small package of not more
than two pounds, opened and partially pillaged. It was to be the
only one. Still, I found sugar cubes, a tin of sardines, cookies, and
the wrapper of a Meunier chocolate bar. I thought long and hard
and decided to invest my goods productively.

I visited the *Lagerältester;* I told him that I'd received a little par-
cel and that since I owed him a great deal, I wished to share my
windfall with him. I was perfectly aware that I was behaving like a
whore, and at the same time, I felt like a tamer of wild beasts entering the tiger's cage armed with a chair and a slab of gamy meat.

I stroked the tiger's whiskers.

I suppose I must have surprised him silly. That a lowly deportee
should have brought him a present when he'd often murdered
their kind by the cartload—I mean that literally—well, that had
certainly never happened before and wasn't likely to again. He
protested like a flustered virgin, a two-hundred-pound virgin,
then accepted the tin of sardines, not without insisting that I take a
sausage in return. That proved to be the most profitable invest-
ment I ever made in my life, paying splendid dividends.

I concluded that each one of these monsters had a flaw, a weakness, which it was up to me to find: this one needed flattering, that
one had a repressed paternal instinct or the need to confide in
someone who seemed to take an interest in him.

Still others—and you had to watch out for them—loved young
flesh and were on the lookout for a sex object. The camp was a

gigantic market of homosexuality. All those criminals, idle and well fed, were deprived of women and fantasized nonstop.

I needed plenty of tact and began by observing my subjects with a cold, clinical eye. I advanced cautiously, feeling my way. The constant danger was their psychopathic instability, for they were all genuinely crazy, and even those who knew them best were unable to predict their outbursts of violence.

So, psychologically speaking, I practiced all the professions of the circus: lion tamer, tightrope walker, even magician. I made rapid progress and learned how to anticipate the critical moments when you had to make yourself scarce to avoid a blowup.

As I was saying, it was Easter Sunday, and the sun was shining. We'd gotten up at the usual hour; the routine was beds, bread, and then—then ad libitum. Everything except going back to bed. The bunks had to remain untouched until the evening. It was the right day to see friends. Because, once again, I had friends. Jean Olchanski and Robert had been discharged from the *Schonungsblock*. It was through Jean that I met Pierre Bloch, a merchant from Mâcon. He was forty years old, robust, and full of warmth. An unshakable optimist, more from a desire to bolster everyone else's morale, I think, than from any deep conviction of his own. As for Robert, he had introduced me to a young French-speaking Greek, Albert Cases, whose family had perished and who clung to us for dear life.

I realize, as I write these lines, that some of my luck must have rubbed off, since Jean and Robert, Pierre and Albert, and even Dr. Freze, who made up the core of my circle of friends in the second phase, all came back from the camp, which makes them as far as I'm concerned the most expensive quint in the history of off-track betting: five starters finish in the money at average odds of 40 to 1, with old Freze not even listed on the board.

It was Pierre Bloch who came to fetch me toward ten o'clock. Together we went to visit Jean and Robert. There I was with two uncles, or surrogate fathers, and an older brother, my intellectual mentor. My emotional void was filled.

We'd talk about details of daily life, buttons to be sewn back on, disintegrating belts, our booboos large and small that we had to try to take care of, *Kommandos,* the different *Kapos,* the block bosses and their injustices, what Buna offered in the way of "organization"—that is, the scrounging and pilfering required to get ahead.

We'd talk about hunger and fatigue, vermin, and thieves who stole bread, spoons, shoes. We'd talk about the blows we'd received and the ones we'd dodged.

We still talked about culture, less than in the *Schonungsblock*— we were much too caught up in everyday things.

We'd talk about the war, the outcome of which was now certain. We avoided talking about the future.

The future was menacing, and we all knew it. We refused to dampen someone else's spirits by discussing things that worried us and about which we could do absolutely nothing. An unexpected little area of tender consideration that created another bond among us.

Our little community practiced mutual assistance. I was by far the richest. My contribution consisted of a liter of soup, on evenings when I managed to milk my cows, and of course any potentially exploitable tidbits of information I gleaned through my contacts.

Pierre Bloch did his utmost for us. He was always there, wherever he was needed. No doubt he was the one among us who'd best managed to preserve his dignity. He was our elder statesman. He always had something to offer, a needle and thread, a pair of gloves, Russian socks to protect our battered feet from the cruel clogs, and if nothing else, a kindly presence on despondent evenings.

For my part, I'd long since resolved the problem of dignity that killed off so many men. I replied to permanent humiliation with secret contempt. It allowed me to endure insults by telling myself they came from subhumans incapable of anything else and not worth bothering about. This seemed a bit artificial, but it worked and did me some good.

I'm afraid my disdainful attitude is one of the stigmata I brought from the camp to peacetime life. I displayed this scorn openly and quite often wrongly. Hatred is an ardent, impassioned emotion, while contempt is icy cold.

Robert was a Communist. He remained one for almost ten years. Born into the bourgeoisie, an intellectual by profession, he was rejected by the comrades, even in the camp, and swallowed one affront after another without ever growing discouraged. Perhaps he was a masochist at heart. Jean and Pierre were moderates; they must have voted radical before and de Gaulle afterward. They'd been wealthy men. As for me, I was a political zero, unless you count a loathing for the style and workings of the Communist Party, most likely due to paternal influence: my old man had been one of the founding fathers of the Bolsheviks, and he still felt sore about it. Although I was essentially a leftist after I thought things out, I was never able to take that final step, and at a time when everyone was going along with the Party, if only as a fellow traveler, I remained a "socialo": Section Française de l'Internationale

Ouvrière, then the Parti Socialiste. I'm still a socialist today, with an obstinacy that deserved a better fate.

Noon had come and gone, a noon without soup. We went our separate ways. The older men left to get a shave; I was still a beardless boy.

There were two or three patches of grass in the camp: in front of the secretariat, the *Arbeitsdienst* (the labor assignment office), and one or two blocks. These lawns were the objects of jealous attention from their proud respective caretakers.

As the saying goes, "He who sleeps, sups," so I decided to apply this principle to lunch and settled in on a lovely green lawn in the midday sun. The constant physical exhaustion that underlay camp life sent me straight off to sleep. There must have been about a dozen of us voluptuaries sharing this opportunity.

I awoke abruptly to the frenzied shouting of five or six *Kapos* and block bosses barreling at us, clubs in hand, urged on by an SS officer whom I recognized as the sadistic Rakasch, the terror of the camp. Our assailants were ten yards away and closing fast. I scrambled up, still in a daze, and ran for my life. My less agile siesta companions were already catching a savage beating.

Rakasch. *Hauptscharführer* Rakasch. Absolute evil. Today, with fifty years' perspective and experience, I realize he was a deeply depraved man. All I knew at the time, as a naive seventeen-year-old, was that I should avoid him as much as possible without seeking to learn anything more.

Rakasch is dressed completely in black, head to toe, cap to boots. His black-gloved hands, in summer as in winter, firmly grip his black leather whip. All you can see of him is his face, framed by his cap and the collar of his tunic. The face is androgynous: delicate features, sharp nose, thin, pale lips.

His eyes are a washed-out blue, and always on the lookout. Nothing escapes them, their all-around vision. They are perfectly expressionless.

His voice is calm, clear, distinct. It careens off pitch only when he goes into action and tries to work himself up. It turns shrill, climbs into the contralto range, and then he unleashes a hail of insults, always the same, based on *Scheissjude, Dreckfresser, faule Sau.* Crappy Jew, shiteater, rotten pig. The German language offers an infinite number of possible combinations for inventing insults.

Unlike the clump of primitive brutes who are his colleagues, Rakasch does not inspire a simple, primal fear. He provokes a metaphysical terror. He is always alone, whereas the SS go about in pairs. He probably makes even his own kind uneasy.

I first saw him at work a few weeks after my arrival. He beat an old Gypsy and then drowned him in a puddle of water eight inches deep, pinning the man's head down with his boot.

I think he experienced intense pleasure when he tortured and killed. Perhaps he even had orgasms. When the old Gypsy was dead, Rakasch looked up and gazed about him, as if to gauge the effect of his performance on the audience. His foot remained theatrically planted on the lifeless head: "Alas, poor Gypsy."

It occurs to me that Rakasch had a mother, a father, maybe brothers and sisters, that he was perhaps married, that he even had children (although I happen to doubt it), that he occasionally laughed, went to the movies.

I'm not lacking in imagination, and yet I admit I cannot see Rakasch in a three-piece suit, blending in with the crowd, turned into an ordinary citizen. I've sometimes wondered if Rakasch was originally a bad actor, a failure who found in Monowitz the role of a lifetime, a part tailor-made for him, a cross between Nero and Lady Macbeth.

Such were the daily hazards of life in the camp. One of the rare places on this earth where you never had time to get bored.

I'd reached the *Schonungsblock,* where old Dr. Freze—I say "old," though he was probably sixty, eight years younger than I am today—was sitting on the doorstep blinking at the sun, which was shining down on Auschwitz and Sainte-Maxime alike, as I remarked to him with that insouciant cruelty some people consider one of the charms of youth.

He nodded; his trousers were rolled up to his knees, and he was busy examining his legs. They were white, swollen, spider-webbed with tiny purple veins.

"Sainte-Maxime . . ." he said. "A week of Sainte-Maxime, of Sainte-Maxime's sun, so different from the sunshine here, and a pastis, a real one, or even a *perroquet**—then you'll see what life is all about. Did you know I've got two orange trees and they're in bloom? Every Easter, I climb up into the hills of Maures over by Collobrières and bring myself back a pair of little tortoises for the garden. In the morning I give them two lettuce leaves, I watch them eat—now, that's happiness. Come autumn, they disappear. I've never managed to find out where they go. Maybe they bury themselves?"

Pastis. Old Freze did himself in with pastis. In 1947, he was already knocking back his tenth one by noon. I wonder if he was still going up to the Maures for his tortoises.

*A pastis with mint.

94

That's how we'd spend the afternoon of that special day, waiting impatiently for the evening soup. I'd begin my usual rounds. One liter at the block plus a second ladleful to be eaten on the spot. One liter from the *Lagerältester* that I'd eat cold before going to bed. One liter at Block 23, which I'd save for Pierre because it was his turn, and there you have it.

In the morning it would be Monday. "Hard as Monday," say assembly line workers. In the camp, every day was Monday. Except, at the calendar's pleasure, for one or two Sundays in spring.

The Big Bluff

Summer is at hand. The *Kommando* of chemists has been working since May. The factory is gearing up to go into production. On the morning of June 7, we're down in a basement, piling up sacks, when a French forced laborer brings us news of the landing in Normandy. He's wildly excited.

We are not particularly enthusiastic. Normandy is 1,200 miles from us. Warsaw, however, is only 150 miles away and the Russians are closing in. What's more, our brain trust is worried about our future. Nazi Europe is shrinking in the wash. And what will they do with us at the last moment? We're in the surreal situation of dreading the upheaval that might lead to our liberation but more probably to our elimination, just when we'd finally achieved an almost enviable position in our world.

The older inmates of our group feel that any change at all puts our safety at risk, and while that strange debate is going on, the Hungarians arrive, whole trainloads of them, two or three a day.

. . .

Mengele is out of work, there's no more "left line, right line." Almost all the transports wind up in the gas chamber: men, women, children. The labor camps are stuffed to bursting; they wouldn't know what to do with more workers. In summer, death takes longer to skim off its share.

I've learned from some veteran inmates that not long ago there was a revolt by the *Sonderkommando,* the "Special Squad" of inmates in charge of the gas chamber. This was the tenth such squad, the first nine having been gassed after a few weeks in operation. The SS had tried to assign four hundred Jews freshly arrived from Corfu to the *Sonderkommando,* but it seems that our Greek friends—led, no doubt, by exceptional men—refused with one voice to perform as required and chose the gas chamber instead. Just the idea that I might have had to face such a dilemma destroys me utterly even today. A few SS were killed, the *Sonderkommando* as well. If sheep led to slaughter start fighting back, the established order falls apart.

The crematoria are going full-bore around the clock. We hear from Birkenau that they've burned 3,000, then 3,500, and last week up to 4,000 bodies a day. The new *Sonderkommando* has been doubled to keep everything running smoothly between the gas chamber and the ovens, day and night. From the chimneys flames shoot thirty feet into the air, visible for leagues around at night, and the oppressive stench of burnt flesh can be smelled as far away as Buna.

By an amazing paradox, while this last massacre is going on and the system is approaching, industrially speaking, absolute perfection, the camp regimen has become less harsh. They have eliminated the morning roll call and shortened the evening one. There hasn't been a public hanging for the last three months.

The SS no longer come inside the camp as much, and even Rakasch only kills a man occasionally now.

Our diet hasn't improved, though, but most of us have some sort of fiddle going and can wangle an extra liter of soup. Plus the work is less exhausting, since we're sheltered from bad weather.

We have become acclimatized. Those of us who couldn't bow low enough have long ago gone up in smoke. Time itself no longer has much meaning; it's subdivided into independent fractions that don't add up and must be negotiated one by one.

Horror has become an everyday thing for us. We don't talk about those convoys of Hungarians, or the dead, or our lives elsewhere, or the future, which logic demands that we ignore. We speak only of the here and now.

The *Kapo* has just told us we'll be taking an oral exam, to check our qualifications for the *Kommando*. It's set for tomorrow morning, and we are to appear one by one before the chief scientist of I. G. Farben. I knew that this day would come sooner or later and that, barring some miracle, my imposture would be exposed and perhaps severely punished.

I might have tried preparing for the test, asking the real chemists to give me lessons in organic chemistry. The idea occurred to me only at the very last minute. I'm going to have to make do with what I've got, which is basically my lycée course and that blessed book I bought at the Librairie Maloine.

In another time and place, I would have spent a sleepless night.

We returned to camp at the end of the day. I went off to get a new bandage, I ate my soup after the evening roll call, I slept the way I did every night and never have since then.

The next day, in groups of three, accompanied by the *Kapo* (who watched over us like a trainer looking after his athletes), we went upstairs to the lordly executive realm. I was the first one called from our group.

I entered a brightly lit office. Along one wall, rows of metal file cabinets; on the opposite side, a table that looked made of glass, two chairs, and a terrifying blackboard covered with formulae as long as a day without bread, strings of Cs, Hs, Os, and Ns. The *Kapo* had come into the office, too, and remained discreetly by the door. In the background were two men who never said a word. I faced a third man, whom I immediately realized was the one on whom everything depended.

He was a strapping fellow of about fifty, authoritative and forbidding, and I had the impression he was not in the giving vein that day. I told myself that if ever there was a time to go all out, this was it.

He asked me my age. "Eighteen," I said, stretching it a bit. "What have you studied?" I was off and running. A speech prepared in advance and rehearsed twenty times. I told him that I'd been the youngest in my year to pass the baccalaureate exam, that I was crazy about chemistry, that I'd also taken the entrance exam at the Institut de Chimie de Paris on rue Pierre-Curie, that I'd passed on the first try with an outstanding grade in chemistry, an average one in math, and a mediocre one in physics (to make everything seem more plausible).

The first year, I told him, was devoted to general, inorganic, and qualitative analytic chemistry—which I thought he'd find hard to swallow, since organic chemistry would have been part of any senior science program back at the lycée level. But he didn't seem especially surprised. I took this opportunity to mention that I spoke three languages.

He looked at me doubtfully and said, "Well, let's see, you're good in analytic chemistry. Tell me something about the chemistry of chromium." I closed my eyes and distinctly saw the page on chromium in the holy book. As clear as a photo. I calmly reeled off the series of reagents and precipitates, from A to Z. He nodded and asked me the valence of chromium. He used the German term *Wertigkeit,* which I didn't know but managed to interpret correctly.

"Three or five," I replied.

"Which is it, three or five?" he asked me curtly.

"Three as a principal valence," I said, "and five as a secondary valence. I think there's an oxide Cr_2O_3 as well as an oxide Cr_2O_5 . . . That seems likely," I added, "since in both cases there's a complement of eight valence electrons, by giving up three or acquiring five."

He raised his glasses slightly and I had the feeling I'd done it. "That's fine," he told me, "you can go."

The *Kapo* seemed ecstatic. He was later to recount my exploits the way Homer sang of the great deeds of Achilles. *"Der Junge ist unheimlich gut geschult!"* The kid is amazingly well educated! It must be said that he was a great audience and a lousy judge.

I learned that very evening that I was among the three or four chemists picked to work in the laboratories when they became operational. On the list, I was right after Dr. Fish, a university professor who must have hugely outclassed our examiner, who I later learned was Dr. Pannowitz, the same Dr. Pannowitz whom Primo

Levi mentions in *Survival in Auschwitz* and who picked him as well to be one of the favored few.

Pulling off this big bluff gave me intense satisfaction. I felt as though I'd taken my first revenge against adversity, as though I'd somehow gained the upper hand. I was delighted, and for a few days the dirty insults of camp life couldn't touch me anymore.

Well, the practical advantages I was to enjoy did not live up to my jubilation.

Some spot-on bombing delayed completion of the labs by three months. As it turned out, we didn't get into the labs until the beginning of January 1945. Mostly what I did was wash pipettes, retorts, and test tubes, while trying to pick up a little useful knowledge.

The laboratory was engaged in the quantitative analysis of latex. We were working alongside three or four German chemists who treated us humanely and even addressed us with the respectful *Sie* instead of the familiar *du*. We wore white coats over our prisoners' uniforms. The sole reminder of our status was our striped caps, which we hung on pegs at the entrance to the lab. And then there were our shaved heads, of course.

Much later, when I passed my baccalaureate in science in a special session in 1946 and wound up in a first-year university course for the degree in mathematics, physics, and chemistry, I stepped into the labs at Jussieu with a small head start over my fellow students.

But I didn't really feel like boasting about it.

Digression III

It has been two months since I wrote these words on the first blank page: *Speak You Also.* As time has passed, things have taken a turn for the worse. That was to be expected. I can't sleep anymore. My moods have made life unbearable for those around me; my ups and downs depend on the pages I write.

I've gone back to the camp. I spend all my time there, searching for my vanished footsteps.

Sometimes I even wonder if by digging so hard I might not be distorting things, inventing empty phantasms, virtual images.

I've even sounded Robert's recollections to help fill in the blanks. He's mentioned names and details I don't recall at all, just as certain people who mean something to me have left no trace in his memory. The play of memory and imagination seems as haphazard as the famous games of love and chance.

Since I set out on this strange journey, I've been making one surprising discovery after another, which is somewhat reassuring:

even in the twilight of life, one's capacity for astonishment can remain intact.

For example, my trip from Drancy to Auschwitz, which lasted three days, a journey like the one Jorge Semprun took at the same time and described in *The Long Voyage* in almost hallucinatory detail, left only vague and fleeting impressions. No images, no sounds, no smells, no tactile sensations, even though I was in good physical condition and not too troubled by an immediate future I would never have suspected.

Whereas other stressful moments, linked to major crises where my life depended on a throw of the dice, left me with quite specific memories: the selection by Mengele when we arrived, my first face-off with the *Lagerältester*.

I need only close my eyes and touch my right leg to re-create from memory that constant pain from my ulcerating wounds.

The odors are there as well, the series of smells—now sour, now putrid—from filthy bodies lying beside me at night on the straw mattress, the warm stink of human excrement in the temporary haven of the latrines.

Taste: the flavor of underbaked black bread and of the semolina soup, *Diet Suppe,* they served us Tuesday evenings and more regularly in the KB. I still relish my soup, even today, whenever I see one on the menu or when my wife (who knows my weakness) cooks one up on a winter's evening.

Why did my memory retain those silly gastronomic conversations in the convalescents' block, the three movements of César Franck's symphony, and Verlaine's poems?

I can understand that when I was at my lowest point my physical state might have prevented me for a while from registering an image, a word. But why do I distinctly see the *Lagerältester,* the *Kapo* of the chemists, the dwarf from the tent, Dr. Ohrenstein, and many others, when I have nothing left of Philippe, who went up in smoke? Not even the sound of his voice . . .

People are always singing me that old refrain: the unconscious that masks, bandages, protects . . . What about those memories of horror, Rakasch and the rest, the scabies, the cold? Those the unconscious tolerates, while suppressing others, like a mad gardener chopping plants and blooms with pruning shears in a chaotic flower bed.

Another discovery, another realization fifty years after the fact. To survive, I'd had to cross in just a few weeks the gulf that separates adolescence, that period of apprenticeship and dependence, from adulthood, when you have to look out for yourself and decide from day to day how you'll manage to stay alive. From a vulnerable, candid, and warmly affectionate youth burst forth, like a butterfly from a chrysalis, that cold and calculating creature singled out by Primo Levi. Helplessly kicked around by events, I decided to become a player in the game, first on my own behalf, afterward for others. Perhaps this was the origin of that vocation as a theatrical director I later thought I had discovered a few years down the road. . .

My friend M. Kahn, the German translator of some of Primo Levi's books, has written me a letter. A precious letter. He tells me to speak, to my wife, my children, my friends, to talk whenever I get a chance, and above all to avoid retreating into my shell. According to him, if Primo Levi died, it's because he no longer had a door to the outside or people to lend a sympathetic ear.

I now know that I'll make it to the end.

But will I find myself the better for it?

The Verdict

July 1944: I've climbed back up the slope, almost to the midway point. I've got seniority, I know the ropes, I have connections. In the evening, I make the rounds of my godfathers and protectors and I collect soup: three, four, once even seven liters. I eat some of it warm, then some of it cold, later in the evening, and I pass one or two liters on to my friends here and there—Jean, Pierre, Robert, because once again I can have friends, a rich man's privilege.

The downside of all this soup is that my slumbers are interrupted by overwhelming urges to pee. I clamber down from my third floor (I've always been careful to get a top bunk) like a sleepwalker, almost without waking up. The night guard, who keeps an eye on the toilet tub, nods to me as I go by.

By day, I'm dressed like a person of quality: no patches on my striped pants and jacket, a well-cut cap with a peak in the front, shoes that are almost wearable.

I've even offered myself the supreme luxury of a clear conscience. An old man in the camp infirmary, fading fast, had asked

107

me to sell two gold teeth he'd pulled from his own mouth. As a member of the chemists' *Kommando,* which for the moment is assigned simply to piling up sacks of phenylbeta naphthylamine, I work alongside civilians, forced laborers, prisoners of war. I approached a Frenchman, who'd signed up for voluntary labor in Germany, and offered him the two teeth for twelve rations of bread. We shook on it, and he handed over the first installment the next morning. I gave the bread to the old man, telling him that he'd be getting a delivery every other day.

Two days later, I couldn't find the Frenchman at his job. One of his pals told me he wasn't working that day. I had to pass the disappointing news on to the famished old man. Two days later, I caught sight of the bastard, who pretended not to know me, and I realized I'd been had by a crook. I hope he died in an air raid. If by some misfortune he returned to France and didn't die of a hideous disease, then I've got positive proof that God does not exist. I paid out eight bread rations. On Monday, Wednesday, and Friday the rations were doubled: I'd eat only one and hand over the other. After the eighth one, the old man died.

I swear that he would have received the last three portions as well, if he'd hung on. I often think about this story, the sole glorious deed I can lay claim to. I acted out of pride, though, so that the old man wouldn't think I'd been the one to cheat him. And if I hadn't had my extra soup rations? I really do believe I would have paid up anyway.

This raises the question of morality in the plainest of terms. Does one do good out of self-respect and evil to show profound contempt for oneself? The law of the camp is simple. You do good when you can and when you happen to feel like it. In all other cases, you do evil, if you have even the slightest scrap of power.

I'm a chemist, *Kommando* 92. Twenty-five engineers, pharmacists, professors, and me, and me, and me. Under the command of a Jewish *Kapo,* one of very few. His name is Hugo. A young Berliner of twenty-three or twenty-five. Like most of the German Jews, he must have been perfectly assimilated, probably comes from a bourgeois family of shopkeepers. Prohibited from entering a university, he remained in his native land despite the mounting pressure, blind to events and deaf to the terrifying rumors.

Trusting in his country, in Goethe, Heine, and *Kultur,* he seemed in all respects no different from the average German. I suppose he lived like that until just before the outbreak of the war. Then the vise tightened. He and his family must have been interned; he never told me his story, even though I was the only one in the *Kommando* with whom he could easily communicate. In the camp you don't tell your story: you don't want to give anyone a hold over you. He probably landed in Auschwitz with the very first detainees, Germans or Austrians, before the wave of Czech and Polish convoys, followed by all the others, as the German octopus stretched its tentacles into every corner of Europe.

He fought his way through the terrible years, the ones we sometimes glimpsed through the words of the veteran inmates, the years before the gas chambers, when violent death was everywhere and killing a craft, when the SS shot down detainees like rabbits as they came around the corners of the barracks, and the senior block inmates systematically beat to death the last man out for morning roll call.

Hugo survived, three, four years. In the camp, that makes you an aristocrat and confers certain rights. Hugo has adapted, he knows his stuff cold. He doesn't overdo it. He's a *Kapo* you can live with. True, he's in charge of a *Kommando* of considerable value; perhaps in earlier days, with other groups, he laid on the stick with proper zeal. He doesn't treat us to the carrot, of course, but relations are rarely tense and sometimes almost human.

Needless to say, he's as crazy as the rest and completely unpredictable in his reactions, which is the hallmark of the old-timers.

I sometimes wonder how to explain this madness of the veterans, a madness that is in direct proportion to the length of their incarceration and that has nothing to do with such things as social class and educational level. Perhaps it was the unbearable confrontation between two perfectly contradictory worlds and ways of reasoning that permanently unhinged them, and maybe my twenty months of deportation affected my mental state more than I realize. Or perhaps my youth protected me: fewer traumatic experiences, more flexibility, a greater capacity for adjustment.

Life at the factory is almost tolerable. It's summertime, a real Continental summer. The cold, the appalling cold from which we suffer so intensely, the cold that seeps even into the marrow of our bones—so skimpily protected by tissue and flesh—is only a bad memory.

A memory so lasting that even today I dread the coming of winter. To me it is a trial, a peril I must weather to survive. As soon as the thermometer drops below freezing, I go outside only if I absolutely must.

I can see myself standing on roll-call square in February, fresh from the infirmary. There are only 108 pounds of me left to fill out a five-foot-eight-inch frame. I rub the back of the comrade in the row in front of me, and from time to time, when there's no danger, I place my mouth on his jacket and blow my warm breath on his back, while whoever is behind me does the same for me.

The activities of our *Kommando* have only the slimmest connection to chemistry. We spend our time unloading shipments of various chemicals and putting them away. At one point, we were supposed to scrub some large metal vats with wire brushes, cleaning the rust off so that they could be used to store solvents.

Since there seemed to be a risk of poisoning from the metallic dust, it was decided to safeguard the *Kommando*'s stock of gray matter by giving us gas masks, and when these were tested, I made the unforgivable mistake of volunteering, in violation of the Second Law of Survival: never take an initiative unless it's in your own interest.

Wearing a mask shaped like a pig's snout, I allowed myself to be shut inside an abandoned toolshed while they slipped a tube attached to a gas bottle through a small opening. I heard a hissing sound and thought, "Stupid idiot, now you're done for. This is grotesque—you've got yourself a private gas chamber!" I could smell the first pungent whiff of ammonia through the mask and I started screaming, pounding on the door. Panic. "It's not working, let me out, let me out!" The door opened, I burst outside, ripping off my mask, and saw the other guys doubled over with laughter.

I'd just experienced utter terror for the second time in my life. I'm still waiting for the third one. Terror differs from ordinary fear the way agony differs from simple pain. It's an explosion, a plunge into a pit of blinding light, an epileptic blackout, an orgasm without pleasure. Unlike fear, terror leaves no residue of shame.

I remembered the first time.

It was the end of May 1940. To escape the coming bombing raids, some of the students at Claude-Bernard had been evacuated at the beginning of the fall to schools in the provinces. I'd wound up in an eighth-grade classroom in Verneuil-sur-Avre.

The Germans were already at the Somme. France was collapsing. Most of the students had returned to their homes and only a handful of us remained, waiting for our fate to be decided.

The air-raid sirens began to wail.

I was out on the school playground, where five or six of us had been playing soccer until a few moments before. I saw the Stukas appear.

With that characteristic bloodcurdling shriek, they dove toward the train station, which was two hundred yards from the school. I'd thrown myself down on the dusty ground and, I would have burrowed into it, if I could have.

I saw—with perfect clarity—the bombs drop from the belly of a plane and fall toward me. They gleamed with reflections of May sunshine, masses of silvery metal spinning around and around.

I'd felt then that same panic I'd just experienced again.

Later on, without turning a hair, I went through plenty more air raids and many other situations where I was clearly in more danger than I'd faced in my little shed with my gas mask.

What mysterious mechanism triggers these irrational and unforgettable terrors?

I still remember the fourteen-year-old kid I was then and the boy of four years—four centuries—later who felt the sting of ammonia, and, when I close my eyes, that same sheer panic sweeps over me again.

To our relief, the vat-cleaning project was abandoned.

At lunchtime, while we savored the lukewarmish dishwater of Buna, we happened to be near a group of British prisoners of war. It was of course strictly forbidden to communicate with them. In the absence of the *Kapo,* who was off eating with his colleagues, I kept a careful eye out over my shoulder and crossed the line.

In fluent English, I told them that my brother was in the RAF. I was later to discover that this was almost true: he had enlisted and been rejected at the very last moment when they realized he was color-blind. The prisoners were nice to me, and I got into the habit of writing out a translation of the German war bulletins for them, the only way I could be of help to these beneficiaries of the Geneva Conventions who regularly received Red Cross packages.

I did it once too often. The *Kapo* caught me, and took me aside.

"You know, don't you, that this is strictly prohibited?"

"Yes," I admitted, looking contrite.

"What did you tell them?"

"I translated the bulletin for them."

"And they, what did they say?"

"They thanked me."

"What else did you say to them?"

"Nothing, really, I only spent five minutes with them."

"What did you write down?"

"Just the bulletin, in English, nothing but the bulletin."

"Who gave you a pencil?"

"They did."

The *Kapo*'s interrogation lasted half an hour. I wondered why he was making such a fuss; no one else had seen us. I was naive. I haven't changed.

He told me to follow him. I was starting to get worried. We both left the building where we worked and tramped for a long time through the factory. I told myself it wasn't possible—a Jewish *Kapo* wouldn't hand me over to the SS. I was wrong. That's exactly what he did.

The miserable bastard made himself look good by putting my life on the line, when we'd just spent two months together, day after day, almost like pals.

We entered the office the SS occupied in the factory. The *Kapo* asked to speak to the noncommissioned officer on duty, and I was placed in a separate room.

On that summer day, I felt cold sweat trickle down my back. I stood there, my legs trembling. Luckily—very luckily—I didn't have diarrhea that week. The door opened to reveal *Hauptscharführer* Rakasch.

He was the camp fiend, a sadistic noncom I'd seen flog a Greek inmate to death just a few days before. One of his specialties was organizing public hangings. I reported him as a war criminal when I returned to France. I never found out if he was shot or if he lived out his life peacefully in his native Austria.

Rakasch walked over and looked at me. He began slapping my face, sending me staggering around the room. Then he sat down behind a table and tapped his whip against his gleaming boots.

"*Schweinehund,* you think you can get out of this? I'll have your hide. Maybe you've got some idea we're losing the war? You're going to be sorry you're not already dead!" This lasted a good quarter of an hour, without any blows. I didn't let out a peep. So far, so good.

Then he left me alone. I've relived this scene time and again in my nightmares, and once in 1976, when I almost died from another bout of hepatitis and in my delirium believed I was back in the camp.

I fantasize about Rakasch when I watch moronic films in which Superman or Batman shows off his power. I imagine myself tearing the whip from his hands, battering him to jelly, watching him collapse and beg for mercy. I take his gun away, I leave the room, I do a Rambo on the other SS guards. Rakasch is much more alive in my memory than Philippe, Ohrenstein, and Feldbaum.

I was sent back to camp with the *Kommando.* The guys were giving me worried looks, while the *Kapo* pretended to ignore me. The next day, the senior block inmate told me that I would be confined to camp pending my sentence.

Then came five days of anguish. I spoke to the camp wise men to get an idea of what was in store for me. They all said I'd probably be sent to the salt or coal mines.

The second day, in front of the *Schreibstube,* the camp secretariat, I made friends with a political, a superveteran, who was also awaiting judgment. His name was Anton. I gathered that he was one of those who had been offered release from the camp in exchange for joining a disciplinary battalion. He had refused. A punishable offense. He was waiting for the verdict a lot more calmly than I was. He'd seen it all, he'd been through everything, and nothing could ever really frighten him anymore.

After every roll call, I was visited by those friends who were able to come see me. They encouraged me, insisted everything would work out—they were going to get the Communists, the politicals, the *Lagerältester* to intervene.

I'd spend the day wandering about with Anton, who was known and respected by everyone. We'd make the rounds of the block bosses; he'd tell me about his life on the outside, about the early days of the camp, the inmates drowned in the latrines by the guards. He was also expecting to be sent to the mines and said that he would take care of me, that nothing would happen to me, that there was always a way to survive, and that if he, and even I, had lasted that long, we'd make it to the end.

The third evening, after the *Kommandos* had returned, I went to the *Kapos'* meeting place, an enclosure near the residence of the *Lagerältester* where they all gathered before supper. Naturally, it was off-limits to common mortals. I took up my post there and I stared fixedly at the chemical *Kapo* that evening, and the next. He finally noticed me and showed signs of impatience or uneasiness. I felt possessed by the goddesses of vengeance in Greek mythology. I wanted to rip him apart, I was seething with hatred. If ever a look could kill, it was mine. He died five months later, cut down by a machine gun in the forest of Gleiwitz, and even today I'm glad I can drag his memory through the mud.

No longer having much to lose, I became enterprising. I wrote a message to the British that was delivered by a friend in the *Kommando*. I told them what had happened and that I was waiting for my sentence. I said good-bye to them and hinted that a little alimentary assistance would be appreciated. My friend returned that same evening, bringing me a few marvels from another world: cheese, cookies, raisins, even chocolate. I offered him some in gratitude for the risk he'd run and treated myself to what I thought would be my last feast.

Afterward I learned that the POWs had all cornered the *Kapo* that very day and promised to kill him with their bare hands if anyone so much as touched a hair on my head.

Along with a few other outlaws, I was summoned on Friday, the fifth day of suspense, to hear judgment passed by the absolute authority, the SS command, in front of the camp secretariat. I was sentenced to fifteen truncheon blows.

My companions in misfortune congratulated me with hearty whacks on the back. They were all convinced I'd been saved from the worst by divine intervention. At first I was relieved to have escaped the torment of the mines. Then I began wondering how I'd hold up to the beating. Anton gave me useful advice. The sentence would be carried out in two days, on Sunday, at ten in the morning. The blows would be delivered by a senior block inmate or perhaps even by the *Lagerältester*. It was vital to keep silent; crying out would exasperate the executioner and probably make him hit twice as hard. Anton added that some thick underpants would help protect me but that under no circumstances should I wear several pairs, which would not escape an experienced eye.

For some crazy reason, Anton himself had not been punished. He wasn't Jewish and was therefore exempt from the extermination program. Two weeks later, I learned he'd been made the senior inmate of Block 26, which gave me another safe spot where I was sure of a warm welcome.

We never recovered the friendly intimacy that had helped me through those five dreadful days, but I didn't find that strange. I'd known for a long time that relations with veterans were affected by all sorts of mysterious factors and liable to be broken off at any time.

Meanwhile, my imagination was going full tilt. I thought about the violence of the blows, falling over and over, and the searing, throbbing, unbearable agony.

Luckily, I can always envision the absolute worst whenever pain is coming my way, so that when it actually arrives I'm almost pleasantly surprised.

The day before, I went by the KB to seek advice from Waitz. The doctor told me to avoid stiffening up, to go with the blows, and to come see him afterward to have some ointment applied. I lay awake all night. Sunday morning arrived. I've hated Sundays ever since.

I was third in line. The beatings were administered in an empty block, in the presence of an SS officer.

The first victim, an elderly Polish Jew, was to receive twenty-five blows. Almost immediately I heard screams that grew more and more shrill. I'd been warned: if the victim cries out, the executioner often raises his aim—in other words, instead of striking the buttocks he goes for the kidneys.

I don't remember what happened to the second man. I felt myself pushed forward. It was my turn. I entered the block. Seven or eight people were there, including a doctor and an SS officer—not Rakasch. The executioner was the *Lagerältester* himself. He signaled to me to go bend over the wooden trestle used for the punishment, with my head toward the wall.

I'd had enough time to catch a glimpse of the instrument, a kind of long tube of solid rubber. I was determined to hold out as long as possible and clenched my teeth on the bit of cloth I'd brought for that purpose. I felt a jolt, as though I'd been tackled hard at rugby. Astonishment won out over pain. The next blow had a more localized effect. I'd expected worse. I told myself that the camp boss was putting his back into it, that he must want to test me. I tried my best to concentrate, which led me to contract my muscles. The sixth blow took my breath away; I felt I was being cut in two. I remembered Waitz's advice. I tried to relax and give with the blows. From the ninth one on, I grunted at each blow, a deep, hollow groan that came from my guts. I could hear the hum of conversations in the background.

With the last three blows, I couldn't keep from moaning. At the fateful fifteenth, I had tears in my eyes and staggered a little as I stood up on wobbly legs. I drew on my pants, trying to avoid any rubbing.

I was nothing but a set of glowing red buttocks.

The *Lagerältester* was smiling. *"Junge, du hast dich gut gehalten, geh dich hinlegen. Nicht auf dem Rucken."* Kid, you held up fine, go lie down. Not on your back. Now he was openly laughing. I went outside to find Jean and Pierre waiting for me, amazed to see me walking. We went to the KB. The skin wasn't broken; Feldbaum applied cold compresses and gave me a sedative. For the next few nights I slept on my stomach.

It wasn't until several days before the evacuation of Auschwitz that I learned the truth about the whole affair from the dwarf—trickster and acrobat, *Stubendienst* of the big tent—who was still on friendly terms with me. He knew Auschwitz inside out, and if he survived, he would have made a remarkable historian of camp life, if only he'd known how to write.

It seems that Dr. Pannowitz, the chief chemist at I. G. Farben, had been immediately informed of my misadventure, and even before I was sent to Rakasch, Dr. Pannowitz apparently told him that he considered me a valuable element and would hold him personally responsible for any major damage caused to my person. Without this telephone call, Rakasch would probably have cut me to pieces. One question can never be unanswered. Who tipped off Dr. Pannowitz? That person also intervened to influence the verdict and obtain the minimum sentence for me. Pannowitz died in February 1945, in a bombing raid, so I've been told. I sometimes wonder if I fooled him completely or if he wasn't duped and simply succumbed to compassion. For the sake of my ego, I like to think I bluffed him.

Pierre told me about a mysterious camp resistance committee he'd contacted that had supposedly exercised some sort of secret influence on my behalf.

The next day, I paid a courtesy call on the *Lagerältester,* who greeted me with full honors. I asked for his aid in switching to the other chemical *Kommando,* number 23. He promised to help, and so in December I made my debut in a lab coat alongside Dr. Fish and Primo Levi.

The Slap

October. A year ago, a boy from the tony 16th arrondissement landed here, leaning on a friend's shoulder to take the weight off his injured foot. A year that saw me sink, hit bottom, come back to the surface, and start breathing again. I'm a veteran, smartly dressed according to the local fashion. I belong to a privileged *Kommando* and live in a block where the senior inmate is a friend of mine (a rare advantage only the rich enjoy): Anton, the political with whom I shared my anguish in July.

Strictly speaking, I don't yet belong to the *Prominenz*, the camp aristocracy, but I'm considered an influential man. I'm said to have powerful protectors, including the *Lagerältester*.

Human nature, it seems, is such that a wretched situation becomes bearable if you can just see that there are people even more mistreated and bereft than you are. That's how it is with me. You grab what happiness you can. And so I've seen dying men wreathed in smiles at the idea of an extra ladleful of soup, and absolute *Muselmänner* delight in having wangled a half-hour's rest. I've managed to make others envy me, so I must be happy. Relatively happy.

Sometimes I think I could have had great expectations for my camp career if only the experiment had lasted longer. I would certainly have wound up a senior block inmate, at least. On the other hand, I know from experience that every situation in camp is unstable, that someone soaring today can come crashing down tomorrow.

In one year, most of my traveling companions have let go. I have but a few friends and witnesses left: Olchanski, Frances, the doctors, Feldbaum, Pierre Bloch, the swimmer Nakache—the star of the transport that arrived after ours.

As the months go by, registration numbers are ticked off like those on license plates. After our six-figure numbers they'd switched to a five-figure series preceded by an *A*. We were now at *B* and five figures. A rational and methodical mind must have conceived of this serial progression, no doubt dreaming of extending it harmoniously into infinity. These numbers suggest tens, hundreds of trains, from which the cream of human strength has been skimmed, leaving the rest to their well-known fate.

The Hungarians were the last victims of the gas chambers, which are now being dismantled, probably so that Robert Faurisson—who is just about to be born—and his revisionist friends can claim in forty years that they never existed.

Last week, to our astonishment, a new type of transport arrived: three hundred Resistance fighters and draft dodgers from Alsace, rounded up by the retreating German army.

The secretariat, where I have a few friends, has called me in to work as an extra clerk. The new deportees are living in the big tent, the way we did a year earlier, during our apprenticeship.

Sitting each at his own table, four or five of us see to registering them. Before we'd gotten started, I'd taken several of them aside to brief them, with instructions to pass the good word along. I thus created a host of craftsmen, locksmiths, carpenters, construction painters, tailors, metal workers, and even two male nurses. Farming and wine making, I explained, were not hot prospects in the local job market, and the main thing was to stay alive.

I belong to the second chemical *Kommando,* number 23. The *Kapo,* some kind of professional criminal, treats me with the respect due those one suspects of possessing hidden resources. I do everything in my power to sustain this ambiguity. I've learned my lesson and no longer go in for illicit activities, especially since I don't need to take risks anymore. In a few days, I'll be eighteen years old. I won't let anyone say that it's the best time of one's life.

The best time of life, I have discovered, is today. And tomorrow, it will be tomorrow.

Our work at Buna is not exhausting, and I'm usually given the easier jobs. The power station has been bombed again; it looks like the Russians will inherit the factory intact and ready to go. Roll calls, with a few exceptions, are no longer nightmares. We've been having a mild autumn.

Despite these favorable conditions, which don't keep the downtrodden from dying, the camp is noticeably tense. The *Nomenklatura* is meeting for discussions, and echoes reach my ears.

There is a perfect logic to all this. The unspeakable years of 1941 and 1942 were a time of handmade death. Everyone had to pitch in, the SS and their auxiliaries, to get death rolling.

It was common to see the *Kommandos* returning in the evening with the day's dead, and every morning the block bosses would line up the night's casualties, laying them out next to the living who stood at attention on roll-call square.

It was only gradually, in 1943, that the mechanism began to operate on its own and the SS had simply to oversee the machine without dirtying their hands. I'm not saying that old habits didn't die hard: now and again, they killed just to stay in practice (the auxiliaries of the *Nomenklatura,* even more than the SS), or through stupidity or excess zeal, or sometimes through ambition and hope of promotion.

A rational mind might suppose that the war's evolution, the fear of defeat, would naturally have had an effect on such behavior. Nothing of the sort. The phenomenon remained purely mechanical, a question of economics, I would say.

Some of these torturers went on gassing victims, while others supervised the productivity of a labor force that was becoming progressively less renewable. When the machine began to seize up and then fall apart, when anarchy and improvisation replaced the smooth running order so carefully brought to perfection, when the Russians on one side and the Allies on the other gradually reduced the killing field to the smallest possible space, the SS returned to their hands-on approach, and this up until the eve of their death, or capture, or escape to the exotic paradises of South America.

How many survivors disappeared in that chaos, just as they were about to return from the dead, while their executioners changed clothes, identities, professions, and vanished into civilian society for the remaining thirty, forty, or fifty years of their lives?

Who knows if Rakasch didn't change his name to Schulz, remarry his wife, and adopt his children under his new identity, to live out his days peacefully on the banks of the beautiful Danube, without qualms of conscience, untroubled by nightmares, slapping his thighs the way they do in those Tyrolean dances performed in lederhosen.

I would have liked to see him dead with my own eyes.

The game is up, but the final score is still unknown.

The SS behave in a random fashion. Some are extremely violent; others seem absent and ignore us. The coming months will be decisive. For us, and for them. They know that we know, and vice versa.

Many of them have been replaced by Ukrainian auxiliary troops or *Volks Deutsche*. Only the experienced officers have remained and those who are protected. The Russian front is an ogre. It daily devours its ration of nice Aryan flesh. Revenge. Revenge and, soon, the end game.

In the block, I have a bed all to myself near the elite section where Anton has quarters with his room attendants, whose number has been reduced. He has asked me to lend a hand in the mornings and evenings to help keep order; I'm a sort of honorary *Stubendienst*. Which of course brings me certain material advantages and some self-satisfaction.

Had I perhaps even begun to go bad? At eighteen, it's hard to know what's what.

Early one morning I inspect the row of beds in my charge to see that they've been properly made and find myself nose to nose with an old man who's still lying in his middle bunk. He's a Polish Jew at the end of his road, one of those who in camp slang are said to *eingehen,* a German word used to describe the withering of plants. I tell him to hop out of there and make his bed. When he looks at me and mumbles in Yiddish, I get the impression he's defying me.

Furious, I raise my hand without thinking and slap him. At the last moment, I hold back and my hand just grazes his cheek. In that fraction of a second, I sound the abyss.

I see his eyes. Eyes that speak of waiting, resignation, contempt, despair.

Eyes brimming with exhaustion, with disgust at himself and his fellowman. Eyes watching the approach of death with a mixture of fear and longing.

Eyes without tears or reproaches. Just a blink in expectation of a slap from a hand. My hand.

And perhaps all this is sheer invention. Perhaps he was simply staring into space, like an animal in an abattoir, and perhaps that message in his eyes was my own imagination. My projection onto him of all the phantasms teeming inside me.

Perhaps it was merely the image of what I had been some eight months earlier. The approach of my own death, of which I had been unaware at the time and which I hated at that precise moment.

If only I could get rid of this memory, sweep it away with my hand . . .

The story ends there. I cannot say what his reaction was, whether he got up, whether he made his bed, or what happened to him.

For a moment I couldn't move. Then I walked away, and that incident, a banal event in the daily life of a death camp, has haunted me all my life. So the contagion had done its job, and I had not escaped corruption. In that world of violence, I'd made a gesture of violence, thus proving that I had taken my proper place there.

The elderly Polish Jew must have died during the days that followed, and ever since I have carried him inside me like an embryo. The memory of my action torments me still. It remains one of the abject wounds that can never heal and will be with me wherever I go.

I slapped the old Polish Jew. The Khmer Rouge massacred their own brothers and sisters. French soldiers tortured people in Algeria. The Hutus hacked the Tutsis to death with machetes.

And in this concert, I played my part.

During the sixties, I tried to break free of this story by writing a novel entitled *The Slap,* a text about another "self," one I might have become, who twenty years later witnesses a trivial scene that ends in a slap. This episode triggers the memory of the one from his past, which I have just described. Against the background of his family and professional life, the man lives through a crisis and its resolution during the following forty-eight hours. While writing the book, I began to feel I was going mad. Had I attempted this too soon? Probably. I fell apart along the way. The manuscript is at the back of a closet, unfinished. The logical ending for my hero was suicide. I suppose I felt I might wind up imitating him. At the time I believed that a survivor of Auschwitz would not commit suicide, that the very idea was unthinkable. How could you turn your back on life after winning such a battle, after showing that insane vital instinct and struggling like a maniac to hold on to survival?

Since then, Primo Levi and others have proved me wrong, and I wonder, whatever could have happened that was horrible enough to make them give up on life? They who had fought back and found another way out besides the seemingly inevitable chimney.

They say that writing is a form of exorcism.

I'll know more about that once I've finished this book.

Digression IV

My ordeal is drawing to a close.

I was curious enough to reread Primo Levi's first book, the one that launched his literary career, *If This Is a Man* (*Survival in Auschwitz*). I had only skimmed through his account when it was first published by *Les Temps modernes* somewhere around 1950. In those days, I was careful to avoid anything whatsoever to do with the deportation.

I am astounded to find that he speaks at some length about me, changing a few details. He calls me Henri, for example. He says I was twenty-two years old, when I was barely eighteen, and he mentions my vast literary and scientific knowledge, which is an exaggeration to say the least.

All the rest is there and leaves no room for doubt. Beardless, polyglot: French, English, German, Russian. Having special dealings with the British prisoners of war. My brother, who died in the camp during the winter of 1943–44: Philippe. My intrigues to establish useful contacts for myself among the senior block inmates and other *Prominenz* of the camp.

How strange it is to see oneself at a distance of fifty years through the eyes of a neutral and surely objective observer, with whom I would have had no special relationship.

He paints a picture of a rather unlikable fellow, something of a cold fish, whom he found pleasant company, it's true, but never wanted to see again.

He seems to know that I survived; I wonder how he found out.

He must have been right. I probably was that creature obsessed with staying alive. "Enclosed in armor," he says; someone who knew how to attract the benevolence and compassion of the powerful, in case of need, "by displaying . . . the sores on his leg." A solitary fighter, cool, calculating, who possessed "a complete and organic theory on the ways to survive in the Lager."

He was a neutral observer, that's how he saw me, and I was surely like that, ferociously determined to do anything to live, ready to use all means at hand, including a gift for inspiring sympathy and pity.

The strangest thing about this acquaintance that seems to have left such precise traces in his memory is that I do not remember him at all. Perhaps because I hadn't felt he could be useful to me? Which would confirm his judgment.

Now I feel a sharp sense of regret. Primo Levi is gone, and I'd never realized what he thought of me. He said he "would give much to know about [my] life as a free man." Maybe I could have persuaded him to change his verdict by showing that there were extenuating circumstances . . .

I'll never know whether I have the right to ask clemency of the jury.

Can one be so guilty for having survived?

Funeral March

January 16, 1945. Since yesterday we've been hearing the hollow rumble of artillery fire in the distance. The German news bulletin, which one of us can always snag a look at, admits that the Russians have crossed the Vistula and are advancing on Katowice. It has been three months already since the gas chambers stopped running; the Hungarian convoys of the summer will turn out to have been their last victims. As for the crematory ovens, they are merely reducing to ashes the several hundred bodies regularly produced each day by the humdrum routine of camp life.

I've become a veteran. Fifteen months of survival, an object of envy for the average *Häftling*. I'm respected by my block boss. I'm correctly outfitted in well-tailored pajamas. My striped cap, of which I'm rather proud, cost me five liters of evening soup. Here, clothes make the man. For almost a month I've been working in a laboratory, where it's warm, with Dr. Fish (a Hungarian university professor), Primo Levi, and a Dutch chemist. With their help, I'm just about managing to hide the fact that I don't know anything about organic chemistry, that I can't work a precision scale, that I've never heard of latex.

I've regained a bit of weight, and aside from my right leg, covered for the past year with varicose ulcers that have finally all joined together, I am, relatively speaking, in good shape. Ten months ago, in February 1944, I'd dropped down to 108 pounds. My buttocks had melted away, a decisive criterion during selections. There were two of those. I made it through both, I still don't know how; men in better condition than I went up in smoke. Pull—or rather, luck, which has a one-track mind.

Now comes the question I've consciously avoided until this day. What are they going to do with us?

Leave behind ten or twenty thousand eyewitnesses to the horrors of Auschwitz? Unthinkable. So, two possibilities. They either do away with us or evacuate us to the heart of Germany. According to their peculiar reasoning, we must do our utmost wherever workers are needed, and afterward we must be exterminated as planned. We veterans have always known that logically there was no way out, and yet a deeply rooted instinct has driven us to survive and to hope, to hope as simply and as automatically as we draw breath.

If they opt for the first solution, there might be a chance for a few of us in all the violent rush, a chance we'll have to know how to take when the time comes.

If we are evacuated, I'll lose my status, return to the rank and file, as they say in the Party, and wind up in some camp or other, where I'll have to dig myself in and hang on. I'll fall back on my previous experience. How long will we have to hold out? The Allies are on the Rhine, the Russians are in Silesia. Germany is heading for a collapse that is evident and imminent. And yet, always, right up to the cease-fire, a threat will hang over us because we know too much, and a fanatical officer could decide to begin eliminating evidence, relying on his comrades to do the same. How will the approach of the Russians affect the organization ruling our lives? One thing is certain: in the days to come, many will die just when their wildest dreams are about to come true. And that will be the cruelest blow of all.

The next day, the seventeenth, I had my answer. Evacuation. A double ration of bread, then roll-call square, if you could stand up. Only the sick in the camp infirmary remained behind, to die, I assumed. They were to spend ten days without food, lying in their own excrement, finally abandoned by their guardians to await the arrival of the Russians. Primo Levi was among them. If I had known how things would turn out, I would have taken that option. But I was convinced they hadn't a hope in hell.

At around six o'clock in the evening, eight thousand human beings, in ranks of five, passed through the gates of Auschwitz III–Monowitz for the last time. That was the beginning of the impossible journey.

Darkness had fallen, and we marched in pitiful procession, fleeing from the night of the living dead. Every ten yards, there was an SS man armed with a machine gun. Whispers passed from row to row: we were going to Gleiwitz. We were already passing alongside Buna, where we'd slaved away twenty-eight days a month, where we'd left our flesh, our blood. Buna, which never went into production, because every time it was ready to start up, an air raid would knock out the power station. Rumor had it that du Pont de Nemours owned shares in I. G. Farben.

We tramped along the pavement in inky blackness. On both sides of the road, we could just make out low houses of one or two stories. Behind the curtains, civilians were probably peering at this Dantean cortege. I heard later that a few of us seized an opportune moment to leap to one side, crawl far from the road, hide out in a wood or barn, and obtain permission the next day from the local inhabitants to wait for the Russians in return for a promise to put in a good word with them.

Others were less fortunate. There were bursts of machine-gun fire and screams in the night.

We'd been walking for two or three hours, forever, wearing heavy clogs with wooden soles in the January snow, in striped coats of thin cloth over our convicts' pajamas, and the weakest began to fall: they were immediately dragged to the side of the road, and a single shot would ring out. In the camps you learn what human resistance can mean. Once again I'm talking about a separate dimension known only to those who have seen a phantom human being take a step, alive, and before taking the next one fall down dead, the last spark extinguished.

The cold. Always present, painful, biting, relentless, intensified by the wind whipping our faces.

Cold. Pain. Humiliation. Hunger. The camp tetralogy: their order—or disorder—varies according to each man's weaknesses.

Cold that worsened during the night, stabbing at our lungs, while clumps of muddy snow stuck to our clogs and made each step more arduous, like a convict's ball and chain.

The obsession with not falling, not now, not after fifteen months of survival clawed out hour by hour.

The distant sound of explosions telling us that over there, maybe thirty miles away, free men are advancing toward us, without knowing us, without even suspecting the torment we endured, without realizing they will arrive too late for us. Perhaps in time for others . . .

My leg was beginning to torment me much more than usual. It was aching, I could feel that it was swollen, and I knew it wouldn't carry me much farther. I let myself drop back gradually to the end of the column.

I felt a hand on my shoulder. It was the *Lagerältester,* the senior camp inmate, the dedicated murderer of hundreds among us. *"Junge,"* he said, "you can't go on?" I nodded. A big cart pushed by some burly guys, block bosses and *Kapos,* was bringing up the rear of the march. He had me climb up on it, joining several of his protégés. Two weeks later, he died at the hands of anonymous avengers; fifty-one years later, through a twist of fate, I write these lines. For an hour I made the most of this new kind of rickshaw. I regained strength and went back to walking. Shortly afterward, it must have been close to midnight, the column halted at an abandoned brickyard, completely open to the wind but protected from the snow. We collapsed onto the bare ground, huddling together to take advantage of the bodily warmth. We fell asleep immediately, like animals.

Not a sound disturbed the slumber of several thousand men, except perhaps the death rattles of a few breathing their last.

At six in the morning, they awakened us. I was not surprised to find that the piece of bread I'd saved and placed under my head had been stolen.

I sometimes wonder about my thief. How do you live with such a thing? Stealing someone's bread, you steal his life. How do you look in the mirror when you shave in the morning, if you've survived? I think he probably died after making one of the many fatal choices that would confront us in the following days, and besides, he didn't have the moral resources to survive: he was already dead as a human being when he robbed me.

We started walking again. I'm not sure how far it is from Monowitz to Gleiwitz, maybe twenty miles, maybe thirty. One day I'll go see, perhaps by car, and I'll stop in a *Kneipe,* a tavern, to ask the locals if they ever heard their parents talk about us, and they'll tell me they're not German but Polish and their parents weren't there in 1945, and they'll be right.

When we reached Gleiwitz, we were sent to a camp, the kind that existed in every small industrial town. Four thousand of us were divided up among twenty blocks. In the meantime, other columns coming from Auschwitz, Birkenau, and their satellites were also converging on Gleiwitz, an important railway junction. I think they let us rest one night; perhaps they even doled out some soup. I was exhausted. This was the first hazy zone of my odyssey: I can't recall a single image, or face, or even a conversation. My vague uneasiness hardened into the conviction that the place wasn't safe and that I had to find a way out of there. The instinct of prey sensing danger.

The next day a first transport was set up, for a thousand or fifteen hundred volunteers; most of our number decided to wait, regain some strength, and sleep. I rushed to leave. I can still see myself clambering into the open car, the kind dear to the French railways: forty men, eight horses. You had to climb up the slatted sides and tumble over the top. Blood from my ulcers had soaked into my pant leg, and the paper bandages had come undone. There were between a hundred and one hundred and twenty of us in each cattle car, sitting in two or three layers. It must have been around midday. The cars didn't move. We slept. It was harder for those on top. The cold . . .

As for the others, the thousands of survivors stockpiled at Gleiwitz, they were to undergo different trials. Three or four trains were sent out after ours. They left for various destinations, which sometimes changed en route because of air raids and track damage. Some trains were halted, and the journey continued on foot, amid villages in flames; the refugees fled toward the west, from camp to camp. That was how Feldbaum died. This big, strapping fellow, athletic and warmhearted, who had managed to become a nurse in the KB and who found me two doses of the recently discovered sulfa drug Prontosil. That's how I'd survived my case of facial erysipelas, which was automatically fatal in the camp. His death waited until the ultimate moment, the eve of the day when his fellow galley slaves, abandoned by their keepers, met up with the first Americans. Like others, Feldbaum dropped dead of exhaustion.

The few thousand left behind in Gleiwitz by the last train did not suffer long. They were herded out of the camp and into the woods a mile or so away, to a carefully prepared clearing. Pits had been dug. Hidden by foliage, machine-gun batteries at the four corners opened fire, mowing down the victims. One of them, a young man of twenty-one, collapsed at the sound of the first bullets and was buried beneath the bodies. When darkness fell, he crawled out and made his way to a barn, where he hid for forty-eight hours and where he was discovered by the farmer, who took pity and fed him until the Russians arrived. The youth returned home and went to medical school, eventually becoming a professor and a renowned authority in his field.

Sometimes I think of those shoals of fish chased down by a monstrous Japanese trawler, a floating factory. There as well, a few individual tuna, cod, or sardines must always escape the net by chance—or perhaps through some instinctive foreboding like the one that prompted me to get on that first train.

At nightfall the train moved slowly off, stopping often to let military convoys pass by. I was in a strange, comatose condition. No one spoke. One or two of our number, on the top layer, had died, covered by the falling snow. We waited for the right moment to heave them out of the car.

At first light occurred the only event of which I have any memory—a precise, detailed, overwhelming memory. We had reached the outskirts of Prague; the train was creeping through a cutting spanned by cast-iron bridges. It was the hour when Czech laborers went off to work. They passed overhead and saw this appalling sight.

Wagons overflowing with vaguely human creatures, neither dead nor alive, emaciated, gazing up at them with empty eyes. What dance of death in a medieval fresco ever presented such a gruesome spectacle?

As one man, the Czechs opened their satchels and tossed their lunches down to us without a moment's hesitation, without even thinking about it. To those workers and their descendants I dedicate these lines, for that unstinting generosity toward their fellow-men who had suffered utter barbarity. I could feel their warmth come down to us with their bread.

We were showered with rolls, slices of bread and butter, potatoes. A terrible struggle broke out as everyone fought to grab a morsel, a mouthful. Half a loaf of black bread had dropped into my lap, and I'd quickly stashed it beneath me. I witnessed a scene of complete degradation. I still remember the grimaces of hatred, of envy, the bestial screams. Three or four men died around a crumbled loaf of bread.

I waited twelve hours, until night came and my neighbors were only half-conscious, before I ate my bread, silently, hiding my face, and my mouth savored my survival. I do not think I would have made it without that bread.

Perhaps human beings can hibernate like bears when their lives are at stake in dire situations. The heart slows, needs are reduced, the brain disengages. Then life shades imperceptibly into death. I spent seventy-two hours in such limbo, from which I sometimes emerged to register a sound, an image, a scene, before sinking back immediately into that protective nothingness.

I must have lived for three days with human beings sitting next to me, on me, beneath me, delirious or dying, inert, some spending their last strength in their last struggle, yet not one face, word, or gesture made any lasting impression on me.

And every one of those men, of whom few survived, had a childhood, a mother, friendships, loves, bursts of happiness and generosity, likes and dislikes, passions, vices.

I don't remember anything else of the three days that journey lasted, except—perhaps—a halt when we were given something hot to drink. Everything seems blurry, like an underexposed photograph. I know that there were more and more corpses; we weren't heaving them out anymore, they were a blanket, protection against the snow. From time to time we saw flames, ruins, civilians whose faces had become as pale, if not as thin, as ours.

I recall that at one point I thought about the trip from Drancy to Auschwitz, fifty people to a freight car, with baggage and food, that three-day journey Philippe and I had found so inhuman. I thought back to the station at Bielefeld and the children who threw stones at our boxcars. Those stones that shattered against the bars of the tiny opening where we took turns getting a breath of fresh air. Those children, who must be sixty years old now, perhaps strolling along new pedestrian streets in the center of town, those children turned into fanatics in a world gone wrong . . . I'm not angry at them anymore.

I remembered that journey and I think I laughed out loud. A neighbor glanced at me uneasily. Many others had already become delirious. I fell asleep. And then the grinding halt and the barking dogs. *"Raus, raus,"* we heard. Familiar music: we had arrived at our new boarding school. We had to clamber quickly up the boxcar sides and jump down. How on earth did the fifty survivors in our group manage? We found ourselves on the platform of the train station at Buchenwald.

In rows of five, at a run, down the avenue leading to the camp. Those around me were as hard to kill as I was, with their souls bolted to their bodies, able to withstand the worst. A few fell, got up, kept going. I don't know if we ran three hundred yards or two thousand; one of these days I'll have to go see. We reached an open space inside the camp. Later we learned it was the Little Camp. Snow was still falling and the ground was muddy, with tufts of yellowish grass sticking out here and there.

The square, as I recall, was surrounded by barbed wire.

Our arrival was watched by some of the political prisoners who formed the majority of the population of Buchenwald. They'd seen their share of atrocities, but they never forgot that night. I know some who are haunted by it even today.

My ragged bandages were sagging down over my shoes. I was dizzy, keeling over—and it was then, only then, for the first and last time, that I stopped hanging on.

I accepted my death.

I lay down on a patch of grass, clutched my sad clown's coat around me, and closed my eyes. Snow began to sprinkle me with white flowers. A few companions looked at me and shook their heads. Someone, I don't know who, maybe a man I'd helped out in our previous life, in Auschwitz, maybe even a friend, from the time when I had friends, leaned down and shook me. "No, no," he said, "don't do that, you mustn't." And at that moment an inmate of Buchenwald, a political, a red triangle, came over and said, "*Aufstehen*, stand up, we're going to bring you inside where it's warm and give you something to eat."

We went off toward Block 57.

The Last Lap

I got up, I shook the snow off my coat, I walked to the entrance of Block 57.

I still remember my first impression: a large area, three-tiered bunks with a thin straw mattress at each level on which four, five, even eight men could sleep. At the far end, the room reserved for the *Stubendienst*. At the entrance, the royal bedchamber belonging to the senior block inmate. I headed straight for the nearest bunks. Although I'd always rushed to claim the top bed, this time I was so weak I could only reach the middle one.

They distributed hot soup and a ration of bread. I ate, and experiencing a kind of bliss, I fell asleep. I don't know how long I slept. When I regained consciousness, it was morning. It was only then that I looked back on my story, back to the beginning. The journey I'd just survived, Gleiwitz, and my decision not to stay there. Monowitz, where my lucky star had placed me in the first French transport that avoided Auschwitz I and Birkenau. Monowitz, the

Buna factory, where I could exploit my pseudo-qualifications as a chemist. My encounter with the *Lagerältester,* and the *Schonungsblock* where I'd hidden out for a good portion of that first winter, and Anton and the block bosses and the British POWs. The hepatitis, the erysipelas, the bouts of dysentery I'd survived, all the stages of my rebound after the free fall of the first months had left me at death's door.

And all that brought me a strange sort of serenity, along with one certainty: I was invulnerable. I just knew somehow that there, in that unfamiliar camp, all I had to do was wait for something— the logical consequence of its precedents—to put me back in the saddle.

In this delirium of chaotic thoughts, I had a more or less conscious feeling of immortality, which has never left me until today, when I'm beginning to feel the shadow of a doubt.

Two years ago, when a big-shot doctor told me categorically that I had kidney cancer, I accepted the verdict but did not, in my heart of hearts, believe him. It turned out later to be a mistaken diagnosis, eventually described as a medico-surgical aberration.

Likewise in 1975, when K. insisted that only a cancer of the liver could have caused the severe atypical hepatitis from which I was suffering, I refused to go along, not wanting to believe him, and I was right. I recovered.

And back in January 1945, in my bunk in Buchenwald, surrounded by my companions in distress, the survivors of a voyage that is now inconceivable even to us, let alone anyone else? I told myself that I'd make it, because things couldn't turn out any other way.

.   .   .

A *Stubendienst* went by the tiers of bunks telling us that there was going to be a roll call, that we all had to go outside and line up in rows, except for the injured who could not walk. I certainly wasn't that badly off.

My bandages were in shreds, my leg hurt. I decided to stay in bed, come what might.

The block boss emerged from his room and inspected the invalids. He was a tall, thin fellow, about fifty years old, a political prisoner, as were all the officials in the camp. He stopped in front of me. I didn't look so terrible at the time, certainly a frightful sight for anyone today but rather above average in our community of walking corpses.

"Warum gehst du nicht raus?" Why aren't you going outside?

"Ich bin kein Muselmann, Blockältester. Ich habe eine schwere Verletzung am Bein. Ich kann einfach nicht stehen." I'm not a *Muselmann,* Senior Block Inmate. I have a serious wound on my leg. I simply can't stand up.

He slapped me and left me to my fate. I'd long since learned that you should never be surprised at anything in a camp. I felt this wasn't the best of beginnings, but after all, I'd gotten out of roll call, and every little bit counts.

That afternoon I was dozing fitfully when a hand shook me. It was the block boss. He motioned to me to get down from the bunk. I thought, That's it, what happened at Monowitz with the *Kapo* of the chemical *Kommando* is starting all over. You're in hot water now.

He gestured for me to follow him. I limped along behind him as best I could, trying to figure out where he was taking me. He didn't say a word. I imagined the worst: after all, I was a newcomer in a camp where I didn't know the rules. Was my past experience, so dearly acquired, still valid here? While I was pondering all this, we arrived at a barrack and Fritz Pollack—that was his name—said, "We'll show them your leg." It was the camp infirmary. He had me go directly into a room where there was a doctor and told the white coat to examine me and bandage the wound. I could tell by the respect shown to him that he had great authority. Wrinkling up his nose, the doctor cleaned my ulcers, placed a dry dressing sprinkled with some mysterious powder on my leg, and told me to come back in three days.

We left; I poured out my thanks. He wasn't finished. Back at the block, he took my arm and led me into his room, where he showed me a cot and a cupboard. "You'll sleep there from now on, and that's where you'll keep your things. And now, let's have lunch." I remembered what I'd been thinking that very morning. Several hundred of us had survived that train and been assigned to Blocks 57 and 58 in the Little Camp. Through what stubborn good luck had I become the first and perhaps the only one to rise above that mass of people? One of the small ironies of the theory of probability. As on that distant day, in the misty past, at the race-track in Auteuil.

From another cupboard Fritz Pollack produced a big loaf of bread, some butter and smoked bacon, and I tucked right in.

He explained that he'd thought things over after slapping me. At first he'd believed I'd said I was a *Muselmann*, which had disgusted him, since my appearance in no way justified such self-pity. Then he'd realized that he'd misheard me and that I'd actually said precisely the opposite. That was why he'd wanted to see for himself and make any appropriate amends.

I lived for six weeks as a *Stubendienst* under the protection of Fritz Pollack. Now that it's time to look back on that most privileged of all periods, I find I have almost no clear memories of it.

I'm certain I must have spoken with Pollack for hours, carried out various small tasks here and there, watched whole batches of human shadows die.

I know I ate everything I could, slept whenever I had the chance.

When I arrived in Buchenwald, I was doubtless closer than ever before to the grave, perhaps with one foot in it already and the other one starting to slip. I was certainly nearer than I had been during the first months in Auschwitz, when I'd never stopped clinging to life.

As it turned out, I needed those six weeks to recharge batteries drained of vital energy; I devoted myself single-mindedly to the task, like those camels whose humps are flaccid after weeks without water in the desert and who drink and drink . . .

I gained thirteen pounds in Buchenwald. Sometimes I helped out my colleagues, the room attendants of Block 57: Colonel Manhes, the future president of the Association of Former Deportees; Marcel Paul, the future minister of industrial production; a few French Communists, who would become members of his departmental staff; and Yuri Popov, a massive young Russian, former national secretary of the Komsomol, who probably ended up in the gulag like all the other Russian prisoners who returned from the West.

Fritz Pollack was a kind of extraterrestrial—he'd been one of the original inmates of Buchenwald in 1938 and bore one of the first hundred identification numbers. He was an Austrian Social Democrat, a fierce anti-Nazi who'd spent seven years in the camp. A concentration camp run by political prisoners, of course, not an extermination camp run by criminals. But seven years of survival, that was just unthinkable. He wound up as the editor of the Austrian Social-Democratic newspaper. I still have a letter he sent me in 1946; I hope the city of Vienna has named a street after him.

Manhes, Marcel Paul, and the others distrusted me somewhat at first. I think they suspected a homosexual relationship between Pollack and me, a common practice in the camps. Any affectionate relationship between a powerful and a weaker person seemed suspect.

When they realized that such wasn't the case, we became friends, and even Popov—once he found out that I was of Russian background and that my father had been one of the first Bolsheviks, a confidant of Lenin—was nice to me.

The Little Camp was a world apart, carefully isolated: there one ate less, one died more, and one was Jewish. On the other hand, one didn't work. The *Kommandos* leaving the main camp every day to go slave in the armaments factories of Erfurt & Weimar were made up of more or less presentable prisoners, not the moribund human scarecrows crowded into the Little Camp. In the morning, even before distributing the bread rations, we had to load the night's victims onto a collection cart. The muddy pallor of the dead, their death grimaces, the tangled, skeletal limbs—I later saw these things again at the Camposanto in Pisa, in the hallucinatory and portentous fresco by the Master of the *Trionfo della Morte*.

What I now find unbearable is the idea that all this seemed normal to us, routine. We pitched the bodies onto the cart, recognizing in passing this or that companion from the boxcar or a work *Kommando*—casually encountered yesterday, casually dispatched today—without batting an eye.

I didn't flinch the morning when we had to summon reinforcements to hoist up the body of the *Lagerältester* of Monowitz. He was too heavy for four arms. After his fall from grace, he had lasted barely two weeks. He was a marked man twice over and he knew it, condemned less by his bosses than by his victims. He was, after all, a monster, and I'd simply been one of his whims.

I remember one morning in February. We were standing in roll-call square. Fine weather, scattered white clouds, the timid rays of a winter sun. We heard a low drone off in the distance that grew louder and louder. Then to the west we saw an immense armada of American planes suddenly appear, high in the sky. They were flying in close formation, almost side by side. Here and there, puffs of black gave evidence of some token flak. The planes passed between us and the sun, and their shadows moved across roll-call square. This flyover must have lasted between five and ten minutes. The planes headed off to the east. The roll call interrupted by this spectacle then continued.

Twenty minutes later, the earth shook beneath our feet as some ninety miles away the aircraft dropped their bombs on Dresden, which ceased to exist. The SS men who were counting us had gone deathly pale. They could feel our hatred as a physical presence, accompanying those bombs falling on that city crowded with refugees. A hundred and eighty days before Hiroshima . . .

Even though it doesn't take long, fortunately, for hatred to evaporate and give way to humane feelings, I don't think it's possible to fully describe the accumulation of loathing that had turned us into mad dogs.

We took pleasure in our very flesh from each plane that flew overhead, each bomb that fell. For us, every blow striking Germany had the taste of just retribution and atonement for what had been and would doubtless be our death.

We were the beasts they had made of us.

I grew stronger from week to week, almost eating my fill, and without having to work for it. The war was in its last stage, the Russians were at Germany's gates, the Allies had driven back the Ardennes offensive and crossed the Rhine. For us as well, the day of reckoning was coming.

The beginning of March saw one of those upheavals in the internal hierarchy that were common in camp life. Overnight, Fritz Pollack was replaced as senior block inmate and sent back to the main camp. I was promptly expelled from my plush cocoon and rejoined the common run of mankind. I'd recovered enough physically by then to weather this mishap, especially since the remaining room attendants would slip me a little extra something now and then.

One night toward the end of March, I was gently awakened as I slept alongside three or four others. Someone signaled to me to climb down, and without making any noise.

Fritz Pollack was there, surrounded by a few other political inmates. It must have been around five in the morning. He informed me that in several hours, at roll call, they would call out of the ranks all the surviving Jews, who were to be placed on a transport. He told me I should try at all costs to escape this last selection.

I was wearing the fatal red and yellow triangle.

First I asked my room-attendant friends to lend me a red triangle marked with an *F* for "French." Then I undertook a bit of sewing, replacing the red and yellow triangle. I figured I had a decent chance. I didn't look anything like a *Muselmann* and I had a decisive argument in reserve, tucked neatly away behind my trouser fly.

At roll call, the prediction came true. All Jews were ordered to step forward. I didn't budge. An SS man passed in front of me without even a glance in my direction.

I had always thought that we would enter a critical phase at the very last moment, that we could survive only as the result of some blunder. What civilization can leave behind the living evidence of its hideous crimes?

I don't think it has ever been revealed that ten days before the liberation of Buchenwald a last transport of between a thousand and twelve hundred Jewish survivors of Auschwitz and its satellite camps was loaded into sealed boxcars.

Around the twentieth of April, Patton's advance guard moved into the area surrounding Munich and discovered this train on a siding two miles from Dachau. It contained between a thousand and twelve hundred corpses, dead of hunger, thirst, and exhaustion.

I often think of those victims who survived the unspeakable, who were so close to a return to life, and who in the anonymity of a rout met death on that raft of the *Medusa* no Géricault will ever immortalize for posterity. They were probably buried in a mass grave by gallant and absolutely stunned soldiers.

Their families mourned them, like millions of other families, believing they died the death of the camps. I will remain perhaps the only one, fifty years later, to reflect on the atrocious death of those men in cattle cars, hammering on the doors and calling out in vain, dying, in the end, on a day in springtime.

Our last days have been described by others. I lived through them; I don't remember anything striking about them. The SS ran off into the woods one fine morning; the first Americans entered the camp and stood open-mouthed. They hadn't seen anything yet . . .

At first our freedom was chaos. Buchenwald was under dual leadership, and neither the American soldiers nor the deportees co-opted by Popov, the elected camp boss, had any idea how to cope with thousands of dying inmates.

Believing they were doing the right thing, they distributed all the food they could find within a radius of five leagues, and I remember in particular a synthetic honey that hustled a good hundred dysentery patients into a less totalitarian world, with the bitter taste of saccharine and final defeat in their mouths.

The Little Camp had become a hospice for the dying and at the same time an exhibition center of shocking abjection. People took photographs of men breathing their last.

A succession of three- and four-star generals traipsed through like that, and the press, and even the population of nearby Weimar. Women fainted, men averted their eyes and swore by all that was holy that they'd known nothing about it.

I'd escaped from that poisonous place on the very day of the liberation, after giving an American lieutenant a message for my supposed remaining family. I moved into a block of French political prisoners, either Communists or members of other Resistance organizations. When the evacuation failed to materialize swiftly, I took the initiative of asking a black truck driver from Washington, D.C., if he would take me to the West with three comrades. He agreed. Reveling in our freedom, we set out blindly across a Germany at war, occupied, and in ruins. We were dropped off at Mainz. An American colonel passing through with his regiment and spending the night there offered us the hospitality of his quarters.

Seeing that I spoke English, he suggested that I leave with him in the morning as an interpreter, and I was tempted. I felt like getting some of my own back. At times I like to imagine what would have happened if I'd said yes. But I didn't.

The next day, we requisitioned a handcart at the Mainz train station, piled our meager belongings into it, and set out for Aix-la-Chapelle. I think we scared the wits out of those who saw us pass. From Aix-la-Chapelle a truck took us to the camp at Longuyon, where we arrived only twenty-four hours ahead of the French who had remained in Buchenwald. Without even realizing what I was doing, I ate my first steak in twenty months, from a plate, with a knife and fork. I'd often fantasizeded about such a feast and had promised myself I'd make it a real celebration.

The following day, a train pulled into the station, not a freight train this time but second-class passenger coaches, and we set off for Paris. The sight of the northern suburbs moved me to tears. We had crossed them going the other way, a lifetime ago. Philippe was dead, Feldbaum was dead, Ohrenstein was dead, and Young Perez as well. In a way, I was dead, too, and now I was being resurrected into a new life.

At the Hôtel Lutetia, a clearing center for returning deportees, I recovered an identity different from the numbers that had served as my name. An identity that reminded me of a nebulous past.

A girl scout who had come there to make herself useful lent me her bike, so I pedaled off into the night.

Hindsight

I think fifty years provide a decent perspective, especially since nature is going to put a stop to the whole thing sooner or later.

I feel I've always been—and still am—an atypical Jew, a nonbeliever, uninvolved with Jewish ways and traditions. I did pick up a few things in school, where I took an interest in whatever Jewish history was sandwiched in between the Egyptians and the Greeks. I confess I found the exploits of Hercules, Theseus, and Jason more exciting than those of Joseph, Moses, Solomon, or Judith. As a child, however, I did endure the horrors of gefilte fish.

Very early in life I realized that rejection and hatred have dogged the Jew relentlessly. Lurking in his shadow. An inescapable part of him. By some quirk of fate, a generation or two might be spared here or there, so that the next one may suffer even crueler and more pitiless tribulations.

Two thousand years of such experience have led to a form of philosophy that sometimes borders on superstition. The unspoken wish to run into some good luck in the midst of misfortune. A humble ambition seen as a favor, a divine blessing.

Why the devil did that blessing fall on me, the most marginal of Jews? Dumb luck can come up with twists of Shavian wit that must leave the stalwarts of the synagogue completely baffled.

My return was in no way different from that of others who have already described what it was like. The family and friends I came home to stopped up their ears. Those who could avoid me fled.

I could not bridge the chasm between us. Drawing the obvious conclusions, I held my tongue. I severed all my ties to the camp: I saw Olchanski once more, Robert and Pierre Bloch twice, Dr. Freze once. I suppose that none of us could bear to see the memory of what we'd been through in someone else's knowing eyes. That went on for forty years.

My return, I now realize, resembled what astronauts would later encounter after a long stay in an orbiting space satellite. I went back to civilian life without any particular emotions, picking up my former existence as though nothing had happened. In the euphoria of return, the first period was the easiest. I was hungry for friendship, for love, for pleasure, for knowledge. I voraciously devoured everything offered up to me by the ferment and enthusiasm of postwar Paris. I'd managed to make my detour through the camps a thing entirely of the past. Or so I thought.

Dashing off in all directions—chemistry, literature, theater, Saint-Germain-des-Prés—I wound up as dabblers inevitably do, with a bit of everything. In other words, nothing.

So one day, after three or four years of messing around, I decided to share the fate of the common man. I began a normal life, got married, had children, practiced a profession. Now and again, in the evening, particularly in winter, after two or three drinks, I'd let slip a few things.

Like those safety valves on pressure cookers that let off steam.

It took me years to realize that Auschwitz had been the decisive event in my life, that a profound change had taken place in me. I saw the world through different eyes, and the world saw me differently, too.

Auschwitz is a fiendish jack-in-the-box whose lid flies off at the slightest touch, bruising the lives of those closest to me, my wife and children.

As years went by, the veil lifted. Everything became a pretext for a return to the past. The Eichmann trial, the hunt for Mengele, the American TV series *Holocaust,* Claude Lanzmann's film, then Spielberg's, the books, all the books I couldn't keep avoiding indefinitely, the commemorations, the suicide of the Austrian Hans Mayer (who wrote after the war under the pen name of Jean Améry), then the death of Primo Levi, the charges against the Vichy officials Maurice Papon and René Bousquet, the actions and writings of Serge and Beate Klarsfeld.

Each event meant a reopening of old wounds, the attendant media frenzy, and for me, sometimes exasperation, sometimes uncontrollable overexcitement, sleeplessness, and overwhelming memories that made me insufferable to those I loved.

That's why I decided long ago to give my testimony only with the benefit of a lifetime of hindsight. And so I had to wait for the day when I could devote my every hour to this deep-sea dive. For four months I have lived and even slept, between bouts of insomnia, with my memories.

I'll probably be one of the last to bear witness, the one whose recollections have "settled" the most. The filter of memory has played its role, letting slip through a mixture of the essential, the incidental, the anecdotal—a selection determined by no apparent logic except, perhaps, the instinct of self-preservation.

When the war was over, I thought long and hard about my feelings toward Germany and the Germans.

I have no gift for hatred. I know what it's like to be hated, hated by human beings who destroyed their own humanity. I concluded that it would be profoundly degrading to play that same game and perpetuate the cycle.

I couldn't help having a few reservations about those who were adults at the end of the war, although I have met some of that generation who were sincerely revolted by their own passivity and a very few who were even honest enough to admit they had known what was happening.

My professional life lasted almost forty years. I've probably made more than a hundred trips across the Rhine. From Hamburg to Munich, from Frankfurt to Berlin, I made some dear friends, devoted and faithful friends who belong to the innocent. No secret suspicion, no ambiguity has cast a cloud over our relations. I would like to assure Hans Hahn, Klaus Meyer, Steini, Gunther, Schneider, Overlack, and the rest of my German friends of my affection.

I leave to others—far too numerous, and often less familiar than I with the ferocious suffering inflicted by real hatred—the unbearable weight of their resentment. I feel certain that what was a cataclysm of history will not be repeated.

What were the aftereffects of my years in boarding school, as I like to call them? Besides the number inscribed on my left arm, which in summer, before it is masked by a tan, sometimes brings me a heartfelt word from a knowing and complicitous stranger . . .

That inability to express my love in spite of the warmth I feel inside, those gestures I don't know how to make, hugging close those I love, those caresses I cannot give—are they the work of the camp or the result of a motherless childhood bereft of tenderness? Both, perhaps.

I'd also lost the notion of respect. For a long while, whenever I met strangers I'd see them in duplicate: in their human guise as members of society and as the *Häftling* each would have become if fate had decided otherwise. This double vision faded as I gradually took my place again in the real world. But even today, in confrontational situations, I sometimes perceive a shadow, a doppelgänger, behind or beside that other person, a shadow I alone can see.

Indifference to death is clearly another by-product. The death of others seems normal to me, and my own death as well. I venture to say that if I were told I was to die at six this evening, it would not upset me very much.

We'll see when the time comes.

The rose blooming on this crown of thorns is that I became invulnerable: the small misfortunes of daily life slide right off me, like rain on my windshield. I don't lose any sleep over minor vexations and setbacks. I have a system of reference that allows me to make light of such trivial things.

By the same token, I take advantage of life. Hardly a day has passed during these last fifty years when I haven't felt gladness, or even intense delight, if only for a moment. I have thus received more gifts than an army of Santa Clauses could ever deliver. Simply because—unlike Philippe, the Champ, Robert Lévy, Feldbaum, Jacques the actor, the old Polish Jew, and thousands of others—I survived to enjoy them.

It would be useless to pretend that there is any other name for this except happiness.

And yet.

There remains a critical point that seems to torment me in particular, while others, luckily for them, have escaped unscathed. It's the question of dignity, my dignity as a human being.

I began my second life at eighteen years of age. Aside from the faults that I have mentioned and that I know to be irremediable, I believe I've led an upright life, one perhaps best described as honest. But I have never, ever, been able to break free of my former existence.

I lived and am still living in humiliation, I have never managed to wipe my image clean. I am still the passive witness of Philippe's death, the person who slapped the old Jew, the boy hiding out in the latrines, the toady who fawned on brutes and murderers to make sure of his extra helpings of soup.

Perhaps the image I had of myself was too flattering, an ideal I could never hope to live up to. Placed out of reach through pride or vanity.

I've paid for it.

I have carried these pages inside myself for half a century. I knew I would have to live with my past every hour of the day and night, for two or three months.

To do so, I waited for my retirement, and then waited to recover from serious illness before I could tackle the job. I was afraid I wasn't up to it any longer, that my lucidity and expressive skills had diminished along with my failing neurons.

Surely it's time to deliver the verdict. And the answer is yes: writing has helped me.

I've gone through life weighted down with lead, struggling to drag along that crippling burden: why me? How can I justify those unbelievable strokes of luck that made me into this fireproof and unsinkable being?

The past has sorted and filed itself away in my head. It is still there, but disarmed, in a way. Officially cleared from the docket.

I'll end my days as the keeper of the flame, and these pages of reflections and intermittent memories finally provide me with the alibi I needed.

Perhaps I survived so that I might give an account, one of the very last, that is both passionate and serene.

A delivery, however long overdue, is still a deliverance.